Smart Business Tips for Entrepreneurs

Learn the 5 Golden Rules to Optimize the Efficiency of a Newly Found SME

By
Emil Howthorn

© Copyright 2020 by (Emil Howthorn) - All rights reserved.

This document is geared towards providing exact and reliable information in regards to the topic and issue covered. The publication is sold with the idea that the public is not required to render accounting, officially permitted, or otherwise, qualified services. If advice is necessary, legal or professional, a practiced individual in the profession should be ordered.

- From a Declaration of Principles which was accepted and approved equally by a Committee of the American Bar Association and a Committee of Publics and Associations.

In no way is it legal to reproduce, duplicate, or transmit any part of this document in either electronic means or in printed format. Recording of this publication is strictly prohibited and any storage of this document is not allowed unless with written permission from the public. All rights reserved.

The information provided herein is stated to be truthful and consistent, in that any liability, in terms of inattention or otherwise, by any usage or abuse of any policies, processes, or directions contained within is the solitary and utter responsibility of the recipient reader. Under no circumstances will any legal responsibility or blame be held against the public for any reparation, damages, or monetary loss due to the information herein, either directly or indirectly.

Respective authors own all copyrights not held by the public.

The information herein is offered for informational purposes solely, and is universal as so. The presentation of the information is without contract or any type of guarantee assurance.

The trademarks that are used are without any consent, and the publication of the trademark is without permission or backing by the trademark owner. All trademarks and brands within this book are for clarifying purposes only and are the owned by the owners themselves, not affiliated with this document.

Table of Contents

INTRODUCTION 6

CHAPTER1: PRODUCT AND PRODUCTION ANALYSIS 21

1.1 Research for a Niche 23

1.2 Market Demand Analysis 29

1.3 Calculating The Risk Factors Involved 38

1.4 Handling Logistics, Supply Chain Management, And IT Infrastructure 45

1.5 Looking For B2B Suppliers 49

1.6 Value Added To Customers Life 52

CHAPTER 2: ADVERTISING AND MARKETING 55

2.1 Building a Brand Image 56

2.2 How Much to Be Allocated On Marketing 58

2.3 Making the Sales 63

2.4 Crypto Currencies Getting Entrepreneurs to the Next Level 80

CHAPTER 3: ENVIRONMENTAL IMPACT OF THE BUSINESS 85

3.1 Go Green with Your Business 90

3.2 Efficient Resource Management 93

3.3 Decrease the Carbon Footprint 97

3.4 Entrepreneurship Sustainability and Models 102

CHAPTER 4: PRODUCTION CONVERSION 109

4.1 Market Fluctuations and Product Switching..111

4.2 Guarding Against Risk 113

4.3 The Art of Investing..120

4.4 Availability of Tax Breaks and Financing 122

CHAPTER 5: PSYCHOLOGY OF ENTREPRENEUR..........128

5.1 Leadership Skills of the Entrepreneur 130

5.2 The Sense of Responsibility and Crisis Management.......................133

5.3 Effective Employee Management 141

5.4 Playing a Fatherly Role...145

5.5 Enhancing Communication Skills..150

5.6 Building Effective Customer Relationship...151

CONCLUSION 156

REFERENCES 162

INTRODUCTION

Entrepreneurship is the act of becoming an entrepreneur or person who undertakes creativity, finance, and market acumen in an attempt to turn inventions into economical products. This may result in new organizations or may be part of the revitalization of existing organizations in response to potential opportunities. The most apparent form of entrepreneurship is the start-up of new enterprises (referred to as start-up small business). No justification is more important than another; no promise of success. However, a deep desire to start a venture, combined with a good idea, proper preparation, and hard work, will lead to a very desirable and lucrative undertaking.

Due to this rising urge among people in recent years the concept has been expanded to encompass social and political aspects of entrepreneurship. If entrepreneurship identifies operations within a corporation or large small business, it is referred to as intra-business and can include corporate venture where major spin-off organizations are concerned.

In general, small start-ups are more agile than larger small business and can adapt rapidly to business or group innovations. They can invent and develop new goods and services more efficiently and effectively than more prominent, hierarchical firms. If changing to trends in fashion, demographics, or ads from a rival, a small business will typically make decisions in days, months, or years.

Innovation also offers an incentive for an individual to make a difference. Many young people in business are improving the local economy. Some — through their changes — contribute to culture as a whole. One person is the founder Steve Jobs, who co-founded Apple in 1976 and kicked off the next boom in personal computers.

Small business are also well adapted to Internet marketing as they can quickly fill specialized niches, something that may have been more complicated until the Internet boom that started in the late 1990s. Adapting to change is essential in industry and, in particular, in small businesses; not being bound to any regulatory bureaucracy, it is generally easier to adapt quickly to the marketplace. Small business owners tend to be familiar with their customers and partners, resulting in better transparency and sophistication.

A small business has the freedom to change its products or services in response to specific consumer needs. The typical entrepreneur or little business boss knows his client base much better than one in a big corporation. If a change in the goods or services sold, or just the operating hours of operation, will best suit the consumers, a small business needs to make improvements. Customers may also have a part to play in product development.

What drives a person to strike on his own and start a business? This is also a positive approach to a difficult situation. An individual could have been laid off once or more. Often a person is unhappy with his or her current job and sees no better employment opportunities on the horizon. An individual usually knows that his or her career is in jeopardy. A small business can propose cuts that might bring an end to a job or restrict employment or salary opportunities. Perhaps an individual has already been handed over for promotion. An individual may not see any possibilities in stabled small business for someone with his or her preferences and skills.

In reality, certain people are repulsed by the thought of working for someone else. We object to a program where recognition is mostly focused on seniority rather than success, or where they have to adhere to corporate culture.

Many people want to become businessmen because they are disillusioned with the bureaucracy or politics involved in going into industry or the profession. Others are sick of attempting to sell a product, service, or way of doing business beyond the traditional market of a big corporation. So why being stressed over new small business policies employment issues or government and bureaucratic issues just lead yourself to a simple entrepreneurial setup by making your own small enterprise by initially working on the 5 basic steps optimizing your business policies and making them simple to be implemented coping with the modern world of today.

On the other hand, certain people are drawn to entrepreneurship purely because of the benefits of starting a SME. Coos became their leaders. They're making the decisions. They chose who they're going to do business with and what job they're going to do. We decide what hours to work, what to pay for, and when to take a break. Another reason for starting your business is Innovation provides a better chance of receiving substantial financial benefits than working with anyone else. It also includes the opportunity to engage in the overall development of the small business, from idea to design and formation, from distribution to market operations and customer reaction. This provides the dignity of being the one in charge. It provides a person with the ability to create wealth that can be retained, sold, or passed on to the next generation.

Another benefit lies in the presence of highly trained staff in all facets of the start-up sector. Start-ups benefit from making senior partners or executives employed on projects below their peak degree of expertise. In the new small business, the publicity specialist had the part of king but simply worked to get orders. Senior engineers were no longer supervisors; they were designing goods instead.

The attribute of the start-up is that the individuals concerned – the founder, their investors, advisors, staff, or even family members – have a strong, even compulsive drive to achieve. This makes it easier and safer for them to work. Finally, even small businesses and start-ups have an intrinsic advantage that comes from individuals who are truly committed and do what they want to do. That is the business spirit, the feeling of fun and enthusiasm that is created as people come together to provide an incentive for more significant achievement than is otherwise possible. This might recruit staff and inspire them to do their best.

Independence is another privilege to own a small enterprise. One survey of small business owners found that 38% of people who quit their jobs in other businesses their principal reason for leaving were that they wanted to be their employers. The right to work independently is a privilege for small business owners. Other people choose to make their own choices, take their chances, and reap the benefits of their actions. Small business owners can make their own choices under the limits set by economic and other environmental factors.

Entrepreneurs and economy

Entrepreneurship is an element in microeconomics. Entrepreneurship uses what Schumpeter termed the gale of creative destruction to absorb, in whole or in part, obsolete technologies across markets and sectors, while at the same time developing new ideas and business models. Throughout this way, creative development is primarily responsible for the dynamism of markets and long-term economic growth. The belief that entrepreneurship contributes to economic development is an understanding of the residual in endogenous development theory and, as such, is widely discussed in academic economics.

The alternative definition brought forward by Israel Kinder indicates that much of the advancements may be much more subtle developments, such as the substitution of paper with plastic in the production of a drinking straw.

For Schumpeter, creativity has resulted in new technologies, but also in new mixes of traditional inputs. Schumpeter's original explanation of this was a fusion of a steam engine and then modern car-making technologies to create a horse-less carriage. In this case, the breakthrough, the automobile, was revolutionary but did not entail the invention of new technology, merely the adaptation of existing technologies in an innovative way. They did not completely replace the horse-drawn wagon. Still, over time, gradual changes that lowered costs and advanced technologies led to the complete practical substitution of beast-drawn vehicles over modern transport. In terms of Schumpeter's early contributions to the 20th century, the mainstream microeconomic theory did not explicitly include the entrepreneur in its theoretical structures (instead of suggesting that wealth can be sought using a market system). In this study, the entrepreneur becomes a tacit but unspecific individual, but it is consistent with the idea that the entrepreneur is the x-efficiency agent. Specific scholars have defined entrepreneurs as risk-bearing, among other items. For Schumpeter, the entrepreneur did not bear any risk: the capitalist did.

Entrepreneurs are commonly regarded as work producers and catalysts for global development. As a result, perhaps unexpectedly, many decision-makers around the world are actively following strategies aimed at raising the amount of entrepreneurship. The goal of this paper is to include a vital dialogue on the incentive and feasibility of public policy to enable individuals to become entrepreneurs.

When we recognize, loosely translated, the value of the entrepreneur in the invention process, we are obligated to act. Built on that, there are three fundamental pillars of successful public entrepreneurship. Entrepreneurship strategies will be inspired if:

- Several people are stuck in employment in developed enterprises that should be better off than self-employed;
- We as a community are more miserable off because of this;
- More initiatives than what we have will fix this societal issue.

Our conversation centers on the aim of bringing people towards starting their own business, not the objective of technologies or developments. The reason for creativity and innovation has long been known and will not be addressed here. To be specific, entrepreneurship-friendly policies are ones that, in any way, make it simpler or cheaper for a person to start a new venture, maybe or perhaps not based on creating a new business concept or inventing anything. There is a multitude of these programs, ranging from subsidized loans or other business expense incentives (such as those offered by accelerators or science parks), reduced stock investment taxes, reduced employment costs, provision of information or other market-making tools, location-specific or sector-specific incentives to launch a business at a given place or sector, to name a few.

Much of the time, we discuss the pros and cons of initiatives involving all individuals involved in entrepreneurship. This means that the policies should mainly apply to those working, as this category usually constitutes the vast majority (approximately 62%) of all consummated entrepreneurial entries in a given year.

Looking at proven facts, we find that most Western world strategies do not substantially mitigate or fix any business failures. Instead, research shows that it saves taxpayers 'resources, promotes those already eager to become businessmen, and instead creates one-employee small business with low-growth goals and little incentives for economic advancement. Instead, most policy proposals that might have the benefit of encouraging value-added enterprise might not be identified as such because, to be successful, they might be more tertiary to launching a business: central-payer health care might eliminate insurance-related barriers impacting job choices; more STEM education might create more programmers, some of whom would be delayed.

Market theory and entrepreneurs

Who is the entrepreneur is at the center of a lot of entrepreneurship reform controversy? Entrepreneurs are a central element in the growth process. According to L the market theory which provides the illusion that there is no need for entrepreneurship at all. Let us continue with a little microeconomics to give clarity to the debate. If all inputs and outputs are sold, if their values are known, and if there is a well-defined processing mechanism that connects data to outputs, then we can also estimate the income of any operation that transforms inputs into outputs. Let's take an example.

Assume that we have a supply and demand curve for product X where the quantity supplied and the quantity demanded are in equilibrium at a price P. The price of product X is equal to the overall total cost (ATC) and the marginal cost (MC). That is to say, P = ATC = MC. In this country, economic gains are negligible, and there is no business entry. We believe that demand for product X is growing, that prices are rising, and that we now have economic income on the market.

The short-term growth in demand would be met by current manufacturers, but the long-term rise in income would enable the entrance of new small business.

Now we have an opportunity for the entrepreneur. The presumption is that there are still agents willing to join the business if earnings are over average. It's an objective statement. But let's be honest, this kind of entry is usual. By routine entrepreneurship, we say that the markets are well developed and well defined, that prices are understood and that the output mechanism is well stabled and that we have good knowledge of the above. Although some confusion exists, no new information is being added to the method. Routine entrepreneurship is, therefore, a form of management. More specifically, the entrepreneur here is the beneficiary of the residual profits, i.e., the owner of the small business. Here, the employer is entitled to both employment and benefits. This concept of an entrepreneur is popular both in Europe and in many other countries. Therefore, an individual enters a market, and the small business does not matter whether it is a sole trader, an enterprise, a small business, or an organization.

This form of entrepreneurship is competition on the market. No new drug has been launched. The small business occurs exogenously as well as the commodity of exogenous entry. Firms work on the quality and quantity market. This typology goes back to the early study of Augustine Cornet, whose principle of equilibrium correlates to the one we share with John Nash today: each small business individually selects its strategy to maximize benefit based on the policy of each other (Aces 2009).

However, routine entrepreneurship can contribute to a significant public policy problem. Is the contractor eligible to operate the business? Is a good manager? Does have enough capital? Does the entrepreneur have enough social money to run the business? In other words, will an entrepreneur reach a minimum ATC equilibrium ratio with costs? How long is it going to take the small business to hit the required ATC? We may continue this line of questioning, but I think you're getting the message. Public policies can help vulnerable individuals gain economic success at a cost. Part of these may be industry weakness due to lack of funding for people in business, and some may be due to lack of small business knowledge and entrepreneurship acumen. Some may be due to intelligence asymmetries. In any case, it is a valid public policy issue.

In comparison to daily entrepreneurship at the other end of the continuum, we have Schumpeterian or modern entrepreneurship. A new business is about the creation of something that does not work on the market. In other words, there is no demand and supply curve. Through modern entrepreneurship, we say that the practices required to build or run an organization where not all markets are well developed or well-identified and where the specific sections of the development process are not understood. In the case of modern entrepreneurship, not all businesses exist or work well, so an entrepreneur, if they want to be successful, will make up for market deficiencies. The filling void and the filling potential are the main characteristics of the entrepreneur. With endogenous entry driven by the research on endogenous technological transition, competition is on the market where entry will overtake the incumbent.

The biggest obstacle to the understanding of the entrepreneurial element lies in the traditional concept of the output method. The guilty parties are the following two assumptions:

That the full set of inputs is defined and known to all real or future small business in the sector, and that there is a fixed relationship between inputs and outputs.

The first presumption is implied in this. The second presumption is clear but never questioned. In the case of modern entrepreneurship, the supply curve does not exist, and the ATC and MC curves are not understood. In the case of contemporary entrepreneurship, labor contracts are incomplete, finance operates under asymmetric knowledge, production roles are not clearly defined or understood, and not all factors of production are marketed. As a consequence, there is a role for those who can cope with instability and for the entrepreneurial organization in the process of economic development.

In the case of modern entrepreneurship, the public policy question is not an unqualified or skilled entrepreneur; on the contrary, it is most likely to be highly eligible. The problem of public policy in the area of innovative entrepreneurship concerns the fostering climate. The public policy problem is, 'Does the environment encourage an entrepreneur to complete the output process and to fill out the empty input markets? This is a matter of information and technology spillovers, finance, and intellectual resources. Some countries may have more robust systems to allow for this form of operation, while others do not. Moreover, given that rivalry here is not on the market for the consumer, some countries could be more hesitant to accept this kind of Stackelberg rivalry that blends endogenous entry and consumer leadership. It produces disparity.

Public policies to encourage entrepreneurship

Public strategies to encourage innovative entrepreneurship as opposed to traditional entrepreneurship are individual and cannot be expected to exist without government interference.

However, this interference is not a business loss because economies do not yet exist. It's about building an empowering environment. Perhaps if we want to encourage development and creativity through modern entrepreneurship, Schumpeterian misbalancing practices instead of Kirznerian balancing practices, some sort of support for the enabling environment is required.

The mandate for a position, whether population, city, nation, state, or country as a whole, to engage in entrepreneurship policy is motivated by market failures and externalities. There are five primary forms of business shortcomings and externalities that dissuade people from becoming new entrepreneurs. The first concerns the externalities of the network. The externalities of the system derive from the importance of the resources of an individual or a corporation and hence its anticipated benefit, relative to a position in close geographical proximity to other entrepreneurial individuals and businesses. This ensures that the importance of an entrepreneur's innovations, the opportunity to find and grow markets, and access to crucial capital depend on the location.

The growing literature on entrepreneurial environments (Li et al. 2015) indicates that being spatially positioned within an entrepreneurial environment increases the predicted benefit of entrepreneurship. Sexennial (1994) offers convincing evidence of the benefits provided to entrepreneurs based on entrepreneurial network externalities. Cities or areas with a lack of entrepreneurship networks face a daunting obstacle to attracting entrepreneurs. To fix the business weakness created by (the absence of) entrepreneurial network externalities, countervailing policies will lead entrepreneurs to find a position they would otherwise be looking for. It should be stressed that the extent of this cause of business weakness is regional and would be most pronounced in regions that have not formed a robust entrepreneurial ecosystem.

Information externalities are the second cause of consumer failure. Arrow (1962) explained how and why information is a collective good, in that it is distingue by both non-excludability and in-rivals. Knowledge created by a single small business or institution, such as a university, may be used by entrepreneurs to set up and extend their entrepreneurial activities. Two factors shape information spillovers. The first concerns the amount of information created or produced. The second concerns the ability to spill over. In the first place, some cities and regions are rich in data based on investment in R&D, human capital, and academic studies, while others have a considerably lower investment in information.

Similarly, individual cities and regions have an abundance of spillover pipelines, which help to promote the transfer of knowledge and innovations from the small business that produces them to developers who ultimately use them to drive creativity. According to the information spillover theory of entrepreneurship, the decision to become an entrepreneur may be an endogenous reaction to awareness generated, yet not commercialized, by the incumbent small business. By using this expertise to start up a new business, the founder acts as a medium for the transfer of knowledge (Clapper 2016).

Cities and regions with little investment in information and weak structures that promote the transmission of that expertise can produce a lower valuation of information spillovers. On the other hand, areas with precious knowledge assets and suitable spillover structures will provide a high value of information spillovers. Economics and management literature argued that these information spillovers appeared to be geographically clustered within close geographical proximity to the information source. Thus, to gain access to these information spillovers, which will, in effect, lead to increasing the anticipated profitability of entrepreneurial development, entrepreneurs need to be spatially situated near to the source of that information. The government should resolve this business weakness by both stimulating innovations in knowledge and promoting knowledge spillover networks, processes, and organizations.

The third cause of business imperfection is the lack of externalities. Failed entrepreneurial firms may create interest that is used by third-party businesses. For e.g., the Fairchild semiconductor failed in California. However, experience, insights, and product developments created and inventions were necessary to persuade not only a host of businesses to be launched, or what Clapper (2016) called the Fair children, but eventually also served as a seedbed for the rise of Silicon Valley (Clapper 2016). In determining whether or not to become an entrepreneur, the emphasis is usually on the interest generated by and feasibility of an entrepreneurial start-up.

This underestimates the real profit created by the location, i.e., the Bay Area, as some of the value generated can be taken and sold by other entrepreneurs, even though the entrepreneurial start-up fails. Entrepreneurship will also create social capital for the web, even though it is not for the individual entrepreneur.

The policy will resolve the concomitant underinvestment in entrepreneurship by aligning social returns to entrepreneurship with private returns to entrepreneurship.

The fourth cause of consumer weakness derives from presentation externalities. A role model or demonstration that becoming an entrepreneur can be successful, regardless of the result, may also affect the choice of others to become an entrepreneur. The market weakness lies in the knowledge conveyed that

(1) an entrepreneur is lucrative and viable,

(2) specific skills and competencies are needed, and

(3) an entrepreneur is consistent with a particular venue.

The magnitude of the presentation's externalities depends on the site. A city or area marked by a lack of entrepreneurship may have a higher entrepreneurial demonstration benefit than a location where entrepreneurship is already widespread.

Sunk costs are the fifth driving factor of entrepreneurship reform. This applies to costs borne not by businessmen but rather by individuals, small business, and organizations in a single city, town, or area. One factor is investing in fixed assets, such as real estate or utilities. Another factor is the human dimension and the dimension of connections, networks, and relationships with individuals at a specific location. By the very definition of the costs incurred, it would be difficult, or at least not negligible, to duplicate or replace such human interactions only by traveling to another location. A third dimension concerns the emotional Connection that individuals may build to a specific site, which cannot be repeated merely by traveling.

Most citizens will be best off not being entrepreneurs. by summarizing the three underlying principles of successful public entrepreneurship. Entrepreneurship strategies will be inspired if;

- A lot of people are stuck in employment in developed small business who should be best off self-employed;
- We as a community are more miserable off because of this;
- More initiatives than what we have will fix this societal issue.

CHAPTER1: PRODUCT AND PRODUCTION ANALYSIS

When we discuss products and production analysis from the view of an entrepreneur starting a small business their initially comes four basics things that need to be considered. Place, labor, consumer, and capital seem to be the key drivers of growth. The developer is the one that integrates and mobilizes these elements in the right proportion. These factors Let us know more about business people and their key positions.

Factors of Development – entrepreneurs the capitalist is the one who initiates the manufacturing cycle by mobilizing the other elements of output. It organizes, oversees, and monitors the affairs of the organization. He is the burden carrier, and therefore the benefit producer, keeping this into account. Simply put, the small business owner is an entrepreneur.

These are, indeed, the days of specialization. But we also see a division between ownership and administration. And now we have a new range of roles for executives and people in the business. Entrepreneurs concentrate on risk control and start-up of development. Let us look at some of the functions of the entrepreneur.

Factors such as Land Factors of Output, Labor Factors of Demand, Capital Development Function The Rule of Diminishing Returns to Scale (Market Function) Production Management Functions of an Entrepreneur as a Factor of Production. In the first place, the capitalist sees economic possibilities in the economy that he can maximize. Then he designs the ideas of the project and agrees on the size of the small business. He must acquire the various variables of development to keep the ball rolling.

The entrepreneur must dynamically build up his business. The elements of development must be organized and used in the correct proportions. Their goal should be to increase the efficiency of these variables. As a result, the entrepreneur must achieve the best yield at the lowest expense from these factors of output.

Risk bearing this may be the most critical role of entrepreneurs. Entrepreneurs face the burden of loss in return for the small business's profits. And situations will change very quickly in a complex economic model. The business plans of the entrepreneur would also be able to respond to the changes.

Customer preferences may shift, new competitors may be on the market, taxes may rise, etc. These would all affect the production and availability of the drug. And the entrepreneur, in consequence, could suffer any financial losses. Entrepreneurs must face these financial threats.

There are also technical threats. These days, every day, we make scientific advances. There is also a possibility that the commodity could become redundant. Or more advanced means of production can be produced. Many risks, such as fraud, injuries, etc., exist. In return for all these risks, people in business reap the gains generated by the small business. Income is their compensation for risk-taking. Unlike any of the other management functions, risk control cannot be assigned to the boss. The entrepreneur must bear all the risks involved.

Creativity, One of the most essential roles of people in business, is always to invent. This breakthrough will be in the area of consumer materials, innovative manufacturing methods, new business models, creative and revolutionary sales strategies, finding new markets, etc. This would support people in business with the small business's economic growth.

However, every new invention or development always comes with its share of new threats. It would be the responsibility of the capitalist to take these risks in exchange for the opportunities for higher returns and better profits. This revolutionary spirit of the entrepreneur will contribute to success in the business and also in the economy as a whole. The most popular businessmen are real innovators.

1.1 Research for a Niche

An entrepreneur may consider a variety of new business ideas and market opportunities, but not all of them are worth pursuing. It's essential to narrow down your options and make sure you focus on those with the highest potential for the success of your business.

Chasing too many growth initiatives proves to be dangerous to your business.

Follow these steps to assess the attractiveness of a new market opportunity and start prioritizing your business growth initiatives.

1. Research your customers and compete with them.

Use market research to analyze multiple levels of your customers and competitors. This will help you assess whether the demand for a product is real and whether it is worthwhile for your business to expand to a potential new market.

By identifying segments of consumers that share common characteristics such as age, gender, education, income, and other softer variables. You can consider consumer motivation as well. What kind of job is the client trying to get done?

2. Get a high-level market view.

However, it is not enough to assess your customers and competitors. You also need to gain a broader understanding of the market as a whole and what the market's potential for success is.

Otherwise, your organization might be trapped in thinking that a few percentage points increase is enough, where there is a lot more potential. Market researchers are experts in providing an overall objective picture and can help you move away from intra-small business thinking.

When analyzing the market, these high-level questions come into play:

- What is the size of the market?
- How quickly does the market expand or contract?
- How many of the buyers are there?
- What are the entry barriers?
- What is the negotiating power of the suppliers?
- What is the value chain of the industry?
- How intense is the competition?
- Is there a threat to new entrants or to substitute products or services?

3. Explore the adjacent possibilities.

A winning strategy can also be used to pursue adjacent opportunities. By getting research done could be one of the ways such as researchers analyzed the growth and performance of 1,850 entrepreneurs in 5-year analysis. They found that the most sustained profitable growth used a systematic, disciplined approach to expand the boundaries of their core business to an adjacent area.

4. Understand the factors of the business environment.

Another area to be explored is the overall business environment, which can have a profound impact on small business performance and how industries operate.

Business environment includes factors such as:
- Technological developments
- Government regulations
- Geopolitical shifts
- Economic indicators
- Trade policies
- Social and cultural norms

5. Find the market research you need quickly.

Gathering and synthesizing information about all of these categories can take a lot of time, effort, and expertise. But market research reports prove to be a significant helping hand. Keeping pace with market trends. It's never easy to keep up with industry trends – after all, you have a small business to run every day.

Nonetheless, it's crucial to remember that the market is continually evolving and that, to keep ahead and avoid rivals from moving by, you must be able to move around overtime for the benefit of business planning in the long term.

Business trend forecasting doesn't have to be as daunting as it sounds. It is essentially a review of technical data over a given timeframe to identify any recurring patterns or outcomes that can be used to chart your market plan, which can be correlated with the general direction of your industry. Business patterns continue to be driven strongly by customer behavior and preferences. Through performing the following kinds of trend analysis, you will be able to recognize steps that could have a direct effect on your overall business performance:

By keeping track of market trends and publications, we don't always have time or space to read every fascinating and informative in our respective industries, so how can we keep track of industry developments? Social media is a powerful platform to monitor the opinions of business influencers and to ensure you remain part of the conversation.

Absorb up-to-date industry research and trend reports like a sponge. To get a real image of your industry area and determine the direction in which it is heading, you need to read a wealth of industry reports that are readily available to you.

By making the most of digital tools and analytics techniques to assess the behavior of the industry, if you're a bit nervous when it comes to numbers, you'll love the full range of analytical tools and systems available. It's great because these tools do all the legwork required to help you understand the larger picture of your marketplace much faster.

Digital analytics can help you discover trends that consumers are increasingly looking for online. For example, Google Trends provides a long-term overview of niche trends. At the same time, Google's Keyword Planner allows you to search the most popular keywords used by your demographic target online and the potential scale for your business to use and bid on them as part of a digital advertising campaign.

Listen to the clients will be talked to. They're the ones who help you put food on the table, after all! Don't be afraid to speak to them and inquire about their struggles and find out what else your small business can do to help them.

Regular, longitudinal surveys of your current client base or – if you are a brand new novice – your target audience may offer useful insight into future behavioral and need changes.

Most successful small business does not follow the crowd; they innovate and break new ground to stand out from the noise. However, the view of your competitors can often give you a good picture of their positioning in the market and of whether they are reacting to what might be seen as an emerging trend. The analysis of the competitor does not have to cost the earth. By only reviewing their websites, customer reviews, and social media channels, you can understand how you compare them to your competitors.

Market research combines consumer behavior and economic trends to confirm and improve your business idea.

It's crucial to understand your consumer base right from the start. Market research allows you to reduce risks even while your business is still a gleam in your eye.

Gather demographic details to grasp better winning customers 'prospects and weaknesses. This may include age, education, family, interests, or anything else related to your business.

Then answer these questions to make the business sense.

- Demand: Is your product or service desired?
- Size of the market: how many will your bid attract you?
- Economic indicators: what are income levels and job rates?
- Location: where do your clients live, and where can you go to your small business?
- Saturation of the market: how many similar choices do customers have available?
- Price: What are future customers paying?

You would also want to stay abreast of the new developments in small businesses. It is necessary to get a sense of the actual market share that will affect your income.

You can do market research from existing sources, or you can do research yourself to touch customers directly.

Existing sources can save a lot of energy and time, but the details may not be as accurate for your audience as you want. Using it to respond to general and quantifiable queries, such as developments in trade, demographics, and household revenues. If you ask customers themselves, you will give your particular target market a sophisticated understanding. But direct work will take time and expense. Use it to answer questions about your small business or clients, such as your logo reactions, changes to shopping experiences, and where customers can go in place of your small business.

Below are a variety of approaches for direct research:

- Surveys
- Focus Groups
- Thorough interviews

Market analysis lets you learn about organizations that compete for your future customers. This is important to define a competitive advantage that generates a sustainable income.

You will assess your competition by product or service line and market segment through your competitive research.

- Strangeness and disadvantages
- Your window of opportunity to join the market
- The value for the rivals of your target market
- Any obstacles that can discourage you from entering the market
- Indirect and indirect competitors that may affect your performance.

Which is why you have to ensure that comparative research is industry-specific? Many methods are available, including a study of Porter's Five Forces. In particular, the level of competition, the challenge posed by new entrants or services, and the price impact of suppliers and consumers are critical factors in this field.

1.2 Market Demand Analysis

What is the demand for the market?

Definition: The market demand describes the demand for a given product and who wants to buy it. This is determined by the willingness of consumers to spend a specific price on a particular good or service. As demand on the market increases, so does cost. When demand decreases, the price will also fall. Market demand is what everyone in a specific industry wants and can help guide traders in the construction of an e-commerce site.

How to research market demand?

Business demand awareness will help educate potential online businesses of the most lucrative market to join. In turn, many small business owners would have to perform research on consumer demand. Marketing analysis includes the quest for business or market surveys, data, and general knowledge. This also involves different methods, and structured data collection process, careful analysis, and detailed reporting. This does not mean, however, that new small business needs a whole marketing team to find out about consumer demand.

Surveys: social media networks are great sites for publishing surveys of goods, markets, and services. Find out what friends and family have to say about a specific need or idea. Submit a letter to anyone via e-mail and submit it to three other men. The higher the variety a business owner will use, the better the market research would be. Many online surveys and case studies can also be downloaded. Be sure to review sources to see how the data are gathered when taking business decisions based on these documents to reports. Some surveys are regional or target groups that they also distort the findings.

Experiments: The design of experiments is time-consuming and expensive, but can benefit an e-commerce shop. For instance, selling a new product at a discounted price for a limited time is an excellent way to test it and see how many consumers are interested in it. It includes a great deal of customer engagement and a sincere willingness to monitor outcomes over time.

Observations: just looking around-physically and digitally alike-can provide a lot of insights into market demand. Observing popular subjects and items on blogs such as Facebook and Interest provides insight into nearly all industries. It can also involve reading local newspapers or magazines in the field where a business owner needs to advertise their items.

Data Types

Please keep in mind that different data types require unique analytical approaches. Primary data is the basis for any new information collected specifically for research purposes. This includes any feedback that entrepreneurs receive from online fans after making a direct request for input. Secondary data refers to any information already available to the owner of the business. This includes any previously completed studies, past questionnaires, or information collected from another source for similar scenarios. Both types of data are valid for market demand research, although the dates on preceding documents need to be noted.

On the one hand, markets are changing quickly, and anything out of year could be detrimental to research. On the other hand, they can provide a thorough analysis of how the market has evolved. This would allow e-commerce traders to predict future trends better and align their business processes accordingly.

Risk comes with all new businesses. Once a businessman starts to develop a solid business plan and model, he must take into account the market he is about to reach. The secret to success is to take time to understand the business environment better and engage in market analysis to evaluate all market facets.

The list below will help you learn more about your target market and allow you to identify your strategy before joining.

1. Identify business penetration points and build a plan for penetration.

Knowing the market and its participants are one of the critical elements of a new business concept. First, you will have to decide who you would individually sell to. Having that in mind, it is also essential to understand that instead of a significant market share, you can select a small market.

Once the target has been stabled, you need to consider how you can hit them. When you plan to find multiple points of entry, selecting a point of entry that will contribute to the potential growth opportunities in your target and neighboring markets would be most important. Take time to search at any possible entry point so that you make the most of your money when making your decision.

2. Determine the primary market factors: cost, demographics for customers, challenges, opportunities.

When designing your business plan, you must consider any potential factor that contributes to your business. These considerations help you determine how you have to target your customers, compete, and develop your business strategy in general.

Take into account the following factors:

- Cost: know all possible costs facing your business. Taxes, import and export prices, pricing policies, etc. If unforeseen expenses arise, can you afford to pay for them? It is essential that you budget your marketing strategy and your overall business in the future of your small business.

- Consumers: to whom would you like to sell? Which are their main challenges, and how can your product or service solve them? What do they respond to your marketing strategy? And what are their strategic views?
- Problems: There is a risk of new challenges emerging that you may not be able to handle. Being versatile and open-minded will help you to face new challenges and plan for new ideas.
- Prospects: even with corporate growth, new possibilities emerge. Be open to new ways for your small business to expand and adapt to them.

3. Identify the prospects of the global market.

Success for business has the potential to give rise to international opportunities. When considering the expansion of the global market, you need to be able to learn a few things before you make the transition.

Some tips on how to prepare for international business:
1. Become acquainted with the customs and business etiquette of the new market.
2. Understand the economic situation of people residing locally.
3. Be an expert on the laws and regulations of the country of business.
4. Research consumers and culture of the country to understand how your product will be viewed by locals.
5. Understand your new competition in your area.

Just because there are opportunities for business in a new area, it doesn't mean you should go in blindly. New global opportunities require the same amount of research and time as your first business venture. Be prepared to conduct further market research so that your business can thrive globally.

4. Analyze the competitive landscape of today.

Comprehension of competition is the key to a successful business. You need to take the time to investigate the various successes and failures of your closest match. Also, when determining which market you should enter, you need to know if there are already too many competitors present. You may not be able to push your product successfully if the market is already too saturated.

5. Define a strategy for the exit.

Regardless of how your small business is going, you must have a departure plan in your mind to be ready for the future. Know what your dreams will be if you excel much. Or be able to address what will happen if your small business begins to collapse. Nonetheless, if you have a strategy in place, the next move will be more effective.

Regardless of the next step, you must be well educated and informed in all facets of the business. Investing in a market research solution such as MarketResearch.com's profound service will allow you to explore all of these market aspects in an entrepreneur's budget without purchasing multiple research reports. This cost-effective solution gives users access to individual sections, chapters, tables, or charts of the syndicated reports that you are most interested in.

You have an excellent idea for a business. But before you make that product or set up an ingenious new service, you need to do your homework.

3 M'S of marketing strategy

The 3m strategy for entrepreneurs to start some starts with:

1. Demand from the market.

This involves the understanding of the customer. asked a few questions that an entrepreneur would have to answer:

- Who is your target customer?

- What's your value proposition?
- How secure is the point of his pain?
- What value do you give the customer to purchase your particular product or service?

That's exactly what you've got to get clear about. You have to be very objective in trying to evaluate who's the right target market and what's going to give them the willingness to pay for your product above all other products that might satisfy the need similarly. Just because you think it's a good idea — that you might pay for it — doesn't mean that everyone else will. You've got to quantify the amount of money you need. The bottom line: be very clear that this is something people are willing to buy. It must be something they need and can't get from anywhere, and over time it must be sustainable. You will be able to answer the next M' once you identify your market and how your product or service suits this market.

2. The size and structure of the market, which focuses on the industry itself.

Define the Three M's here are the things to consider before embarking on a business: market demand: decide who your clients are. Are they at hand? They're open, huh? So many are there?

Size and structure of the market: is the industry fragmented or emerging? What are your rivals, and what are your strategic and sustainable advantages?

Money: How much does a reasonable or service cost? Can you make a profit by paying enough? Do you have the cash flow that you need to support the launch of your business?

Don't think your small business is so fresh or exclusive that you won't have any rivals, warns. You will have competition, and you have to figure out who your competition is, even in the local market. You have to differentiate your product by having a sustainable competitive advantage so that consumers switch from where they get their products right now. Knowing market demand, scale, and structure, you can launch your startup with the third and final key.

3. How much does the development of this kind or service cost me and will I charge enough money to make it?

The sales at the end of the day, minus the product expenses, will be about 40 percent or more. If you need to be able to get your operating costs up, you want at least a respectable gross margin. The connection is how long it would take to get your small business going. Suppose it would cost $10,000, but you only lost 20% of your portfolio. Could you afford $10,000 to invest in this small business? The calculation of the start-up costs also forms part of the margin analysis when the potential is evaluated,

notes that monetary considerations should not be taken lightly. It takes longer than you expect, it's a lot easier to work than you expect, cost more than you think, and people will choose to pay less than you think. Anything would have an effect on your balance.

Let's say it's your business 'first day. Early 60 days, you can file documents, print business cards, and create a website. You'll network and make contact next month, but you've got no sales. You are here, from 90 to 120 days, and have yet to produce any profits. A lot of entrepreneurs would underestimate the amount of time that it takes to start a small business and produce a small amount of revenue. So, I also recommend that if you cannot help yourself for at least one year – and you don't get it at the bank – you've been putting yourself at risk. Will you still have enough cash flow when you sell a product and produce revenue to receive receipts and support your operation? Is calling for it. Money flow awareness is even more important now, because access to credit will not work as well in the economic downturn. And now, women need to be even more mindful about and appreciate what their cash flow needs are. Networking is becoming increasingly necessary. To have a link with decision-making. You must call that person; you must meet that person; they must connect with you in a way that is not the traditional way. The authors explain in this condensed extract the importance of market analysis to get knowledge on the three relevant fields you will have to explore before your new small business is launched. So you have a good idea for a product — something which is expected to catch customers 'hearts and minds (and wallets) everywhere. Or maybe you have stumbled on a service nobody else offers — one that's badly needed. This is your chance! Do not hesitate ... Don't ... Don't look back ... doesn't look back ... Spring into it right now and ... Wait! Until you switch to high gear, you have to decide if your product or service is on the market. Not only that, but you also need to find out what, if any, is needed for fine-tuning. Simply put, you have to do market research. Most business owners, for the sole reason, that they do not want to hear negative reviews ignore this critical phase in product growth. You are persuaded that the product or service is just as good as it is, and you don't want to compromise it. Many people in business avoid market analysis because they think it'll be too expensive. It is not easy to justify wasting money on research at all other start-up costs that reveal just what you have known all the time: the small business is a winner. Regardless of why market research failure will lead to a death penalty for your small business. A lot of businesses miss essential context information because they are so keen to sell their product. But the best businesses do their homework. Find market analysis as a potential investment. And what is consumer research exactly? Simply put, this is a way to gather the information that you can use to fix or avoid marketing issues. Good market analysis provides you with the knowledge you need to create a marketing strategy that works for you. You may define the specific segments within a market that you want to reach and establish a product or service brand that distinguish you from your competitors. Market research can also help you find the best location to start your new small business. These sources will provide feedback and help you with your first market research step: to determine exactly what information you need to collect. Market research will, in general, give you details on three main areas:

Data from the industry. Look for the emerging developments in market analysis. Compare industry statistics and production. What sectors continue to grow, and which are declining? Will the market work for new consumer types? Which are the technical advances in the industry? Why do you benefit from them? A thriving, stable industry is key; you don't want to start a new business in a field that's on the decline.

Consumer close-up. Your market research on the customer side will start with a market survey. A comprehensive market survey allows you to make a realistic sales prediction for your new product. To perform a market survey, you first have to assess the market limits or physical limits in the area you sell. First, research the population's spending characteristics in this area. Estimate the buying power of the region on the basis of per capita income, medium income, unemployment rate, population, and others. Determine the current sales volume for the product or service form you are selling in the region. Finally, determine how far you can realistically reach the overall sales value.

Close-up rivalry. A better view of the market will emerge on the basis of a mix of business research and customer research. Don't underestimate the number of participants out there. Hold an eye on possible future and existing rivals. Examine the number of competitors at a local and, where applicable, national level. Study their tactics and practices. Your research will give you a good picture of your new business 'future risks, opportunities, and market vulnerabilities and strengths. When you look at the market, try to see which patterns in the industry were created and whether your business has an opportunity or an advantage. For research, rivals use the library, the Internet, and other secondary research outlets. Read as many papers as possible about the businesses in which you will work. When you are looking for businesses that are publicly owned, contact them to receive copies of their annual reports. They also demonstrate not only the progress of a business but also what goods or services it plans to underline in the future.

1.3 Calculating The Risk Factors Involved

If you're looking for ways to develop in business or marketing, a calculated risk- may be your answer. This process is essential for entrepreneurs and business owners alike. You're not going to be tempted to push the boundaries or question the status quo if you keep it safe. Keep in mind that it's impossible to predict how your calculated risk will work out. However, much as a decision might lead to possible progress, there is always a chance for disappointment. There are essential actions you should take to reduce confusion or costs. If you decide the time to learn these moves, consider the drawbacks of risk, and see how many have achieved it, you can find that you can come up with one of your own.

What's the calculated risk?

The calculated risk is a risk that is deliberately prepared and focused on careful analysis of the possible risks and benefits. Determined risk-takers develop their goals and the actions they must follow to reach them. Instead of tossing the dice, they consider ways to reduce the chance so that their dream is in line with reality.

Bear in mind that any business decision has its own set of advantages and disadvantages. When you lower your limits by taking the chance you measure, certain variables increase significantly. Once you think accordingly, you will build up a strategy and a schedule that has more potential for success.

Do Your Due Diligence Choices which should not be dependent on feelings. Instead, explain your ideas in reasoning and analyze every detail. Break down the decision to make more choices so that you don't get frustrated by chance. Such smaller options are individual challenges that contribute to the ultimate target. Alternatively, evaluate all potential routes to figure out which direction is most effective.

You can't afford to check the information that you believe is minor. One helpful suggestion is to ask the opinion of a reliable lawyer. Invest time by reading through all the numbers, so you don't have to rush last minute to correct any errors.

When you contact a trustworthy partner, each of you will point out some red flags or future problems before they emerge. Any excellent questioning questions that need to be answered include:

- if a contract loses money, how does the small business respond?
- if a relationship breaks down, what sort of steps are you going to take?
- if the proposal is late, how are you going to reach the deadline?

Think Will the bottom line continue to take some losses if the chance you've been waiting for starts to fail? When you dial and keep track of the numbers that go into your measured risk, which is able to determine the success of the plan.

It's a smart thing to find a coach, too. Introduce them to the proposal and action plan so that they can point out any shortcomings or errors they may have made in the past. Years of disappointment at their end will save you precious time on your path to success.

Checkpoints

It's time to build a road map after you take the time and resources to compile all the useful knowledge you need. Develop a well-built action plan, along with a list of potential outcomes. Don't take chances, and you're going to be able to figure exactly how the opportunity is going to be.

Although you could be working months or years ahead of your ideal goal, frequent reminders will keep you focused on keeping the course.

Jump

When you feel right. Don't forget your work and results. You've got to focus on them, and they're going to find out where the right moment happens to take the plunge.

This being, it's all right to say no. Not every plan can be followed, which is why you will stress the importance of setting down the groundwork and the actions that you should take. It's hard to explore an unlikely or surprising prospect if the plate is already full.

Be Ready to Pivot.

You may need to revise your well-planned strategy. The budget may be cut, and the relationship may collapse. Your plan is good if it gives you the flexibility to change course and keep your thinking forward.

Let's assume you're pursuing a new $50,000 project plan. Two months into a four-month project, you'll find that your budget is being cut by $10,000. What are you doing? For a smart strategy, you will go back to the drawing board and bring together a new approach.

Benefits of Measured Risk

By taking calculated risks and not going All In on all the innovations, entrepreneurs can avoid sabotaging their small business growth. Nothing remarkable happens to people who are so dull and do not invent. The measured chance sends you out of the ordinary. Even if your idea turns into a colossal flop, you're going to evolve from your ability to try something different. Time isn't lost; it's a way for you to learn how to change next time.

Competitive advantage

The demands of the competition are always changing. When they do, the underlying interests and was of the clients will grow. They need a new feature. If you're the one who has the guts to give it to them, you're going to be praised. Not only will these consumers recall your small business, but they will distribute references to provide you with a robust market.

Shift the market Being mediocre and sticking to the status quo won't make it down in today's economy. To keep ahead of the race, you're going to have to come up with ideas and do something that others aren't able to do.

Crush the fear of disappointment. Once you take the plunge and figure out that the challenge has made you through, you will be open to more possibilities. Everything else is you capable of doing? When you can crack down the misconception of your boundaries, how else can you get better?

Learn to Depend On Others and Trust Them By removing your worries; you can learn to appreciate and trust the cycle that has brought you there. The colleagues and the close business friends are there to work with you should you need an additional boost in confidence.

Characteristics of the risk-taker

The attributes of the risk-taker are as follows:

1. Optimistic about the possibilities – Hope doesn't just make you feel better; it helps you feel more comfortable. As a leader or an entrepreneur, trusting in your decisions is vital, especially when others follow you.

2. Comfortable taking chances – Whether you're seeking a potential strategic relationship or developing a new idea in your wheelhouse, taking risks is where innovation takes place. The more risks you choose, the more confident you will feel.

3. Agile and ready to adjust – If there is uncertainty, it is essential to take steps and brace oneself for any possible result. When a new business idea or initiative does not go as expected, be able to change and pivot.

4. Focused on implementation – The implementation of an idea or proposal is almost as critical as planning and preparing. Have a squad in position to help you out. A good team will build the action plan you want and establish Plan B if the strategy doesn't go well.

These traits do not necessarily come quickly and can be experienced by experience. Try seeking a mentor in your business that will coach you and direct you along the way. A coach may offer insight into the mistakes that may have been made. So, how and why do you take measured chances as an entrepreneur? Calculated danger takes a tremendous amount of time, effort, and bravery. Your decisions are of considerable significance to the future of your small business. If you are working on a strategic strategy to carry out your measured risk, you are opening the door to real creativity and success for your small business. Master these moves; the rewards of every day of your life may be included in the list of innovators who overcome the odds

1. Cash balance control is essential to this. Most startups fail for several causes, but one of them is much more popular than the others — run out of capital. We need to know where a single dollar comes from and where a unique sound comes from. If you don't prioritize your cash flow, you're going to put your small business in a dangerous place. It doesn't matter how good the plan could be if you run out of the money you hit a brick wall. Place the budget and hold to it.

2. Log and control all spending. For a new startup, there are going to cost flowing from both angles to you. Hiring a full-time worker to oversee accounts at the outset is not so budget-friendly, so use accounting tools to keep coordinated.

   Not only does this assist in cash flow control, but it also makes it much easier for the tax to be paid every year. When you expand, and the accounting system gets more complicated, you may need to consider recruiting an expert.

3. Reduce the fixed costs at the outset. At the beginning of the start-up process, keeping the costs down is the secret to sustainability. You don't need a large, lavish office in the center of your city or a freshly catered meal three times a day. Operate thin enough that you can devote the majority of your resources to production, which will allow you to make whatever profit you want one day. So many entrepreneurs depend on the wrong things — like luxurious workplaces and over-the-top amenities — and forget that producing sales will be their top goal. Remain hopeful, but be prepared for the worst.

4. You never know what happens when you start a small business, so it's best to brace yourself for the worst possible scenario. Don't leave your work and remove

your crucial source of revenue before your small business is ready to substitute that money.

Hold the reserves — both personal and business — in the emergency savings account. You will never be too prepared for a difficult scenario. Sadly, they do happen, sometimes when you least want them to happen. As an entrepreneur, you are responsible for your retirement, so when you start making money, find stuff like a Roth IRA and some savings, even small ones. Anything is better than nothing — consider micro-investment incentives or distribute funds every month to an online marketplace like E*TRADE.

5. Every minute of your time is worth it. You are going to make it short and sweet: time is money. Nothing's worth more than your time. You just have so much of it every day, so take it into account when preparing your day and day-to-day activities. Any second you spent doing something that isn't relevant to your small business is time (and money) lost.

6. Based on the retention of the client. You don't have a market without clients. As soon as we learn to acquire customers and scale, the higher your small business's chances are. When you have defined various procurement platforms, focus on efficiency to reduce the costs. It is impractical to check any potential acquisition channel at first, both in terms of time and expense, so concentrate on the most profitable opportunities. If you've scaled them effectively, you'll have the financial resources to pursue other platforms.

7. Make sure you're paying attention. Your hard work and commitment to your small business alone will not bring food on the table — you need to provide for yourself. Although you don't have to give yourself a

huge, fat paycheck at the outset, make sure you spend enough to survive.

Give yourself enough to live comfortably and concentrate on building your firm. By removing personal financial tension, you can remain ultra-focused on your small business. You can't eat your ramen noodles forever. Give yourself a little padding and warmth.

8. Establish financial targets. Instead of merely saying, I want to create a multi-million dollar corporation, you need to break down the financial targets into concrete and observable ones. Monthly, weekly, or even regular sales goals help you to keep on track and make the changes required for consistent growth. You can also set targets to hit along the way, allowing you a lot of smaller goals to keep on reaching. Knocking out small targets will give you the trust you need to hold control on your entrepreneurial path.

1.4 Handling Logistics, Supply Chain Management, And IT Infrastructure

Logistics has, by far, been one of the most important and yet one of the least relevant roles in all market settings, often perceived to be an 'operational' role rather than a strategic one. As a result, it remained a shoddy ability work that was an additional / on-the-side task performed by those in management or accounting, and never by procurement or supply chain specialists. Learning from their mentor, they will receive quotes, book a shipment, and track/update those stakeholders on the successful completion of the process.

Recently, through the advent of technologies and automated systems as well as new policy policies, businesses work based on a mindset that demands a year-on-year decrease in

Logistics costs. It is essential, though, to look at the traditional modus operandi; this transition is generally orchestrated by upper management as part of their budgets and board meetings, which are often supervised by entrepreneurs themselves. However, the person who supports the proposals, the financial planner, and the real developer of the plan never sits in the same room, resulting in a massive gap and failure to deliver the desired results.

Reverse Auctions and RFQs are very popular today; it is easy to understand how well versed the Supply Chain consumer is after having engaged in many and working with consumers on their specifications. The definition of Total Cost of Ownership (TCO) is not widespread, and thus the relaying of the AS-IS and TO-BE conditions is not emphasized at the time of the RFQ. Also, service providers quote aggressive pricing based on the information provided and, at the time of delivery, inconsistency results in lower performance levels to save costs but also more reduced customer satisfaction. With this disconnect, it reminds me of Terry Pritchett's clichéd and appropriate quotation, They say a little information is a risky thing, but it's not a half as bad as a lot of ignorance. They still say you can't change the world until you change yourself from within, that's always true when you're trying to improve your service provider. The questions that should be posted first of all are not in any particular order:

1. Why should I contest the status quo?
2. Is that what drives my current strategy?
3. Which are the pressure points that I did not discuss with my friend (service provider)?
4. Was my LSP capable of adjusting to the shift in my requirements?
5. Could we change the way we've worked all these years?

6. Am I going to push transition, or am I deputizing for someone who has the expertise to do it?
7. Have I recruited the right person to do the work internally and externally?
8. When I make a move, am I able to pay for it? What is the impact on my Manufacturing? Delivery, huh? Purchase of raw materials?
9. Why does this move affect my customer?

There is a bundle of questions that need to be resolved, so that needs to be achieved through clear discussion, because even though you don't know the solutions, it doesn't make sense to consult with someone who can help you come to that conclusion. There are some exceptionally talented Purchase & Supply Chain executives who work to make incredible improvements to supply chains, but then again, they're not the bulk. Something further to talk of when gazing at the current enterprise can be further discussed below with a few insightful points as to why one can look about implementing improvements and where the profit factor generates efficiencies and cost reductions, which leads the business plan.

How Important is a Market Effective SCM?

The active role of the Supply and/or Demand Chain department is at the heart of the market for small business in Foreign Trading, FMCG, E-Commerce, and domestic customer consumption. In such a scenario, outsourcing the task to a 3PL/4PL specialist who can guarantee quality and cost-effective service will be of value to the bottom line but, most significantly, to customer loyalty. When designing a personalized solution for your small business, it is essential to analyze the long-term effect and not only place band help on the immediate need, because it is a buzz word.

Are key market competencies optimized?

Currently, most small business are looking at developing the Supply Chain internally; as this gives them efficiency, power, and usability advantages, the process of designing, setting up, and managing ancillary set-up will potentially absorb vital resources and undermine the emphasis and performance of their core competencies. Often, more substantial conglomerates and MNCs, who possess a diversified market portfolio and may hire qualified personnel to handle each feature, tend to create an in-house SCM process that complements their core competencies.

However, in the case of other firms not limited to start-ups or small and medium-sized enterprises and first-generation entrepreneurs, incurring increased expenses and diving capital to operate an in-house SCM activity may be counter-productive and counterproductive to the small business. Thus, in addition to determining the value of logistics and SCM for the small business, it is also essential to evaluate the availability of services and how the core competencies of the small business will be compromised by the in-house set-up.

Does the SCM feature have a significant effect on consumer satisfaction?

They are emulating the E-Commerce form of customer interaction and fulfillment on the same day or the next day of delivery, even though it is necessary for the B2B product to arrive at a high cost. Forecasting market demand and sufficient massive inventory keeping costs will guarantee that, but is it something that industries outside Automotive and Aviation are doing today?

Knowing what the consumer wants should decide whether to organize the supply chain and, if there is little consistency in coordination and planning, that can lead to a bullwhip result that is counter-intuitive to the supply chain potential. There are other aspects of Just in Time and Lean to be discussed later but knowing what the consumer wants / needs depending on the actuality and not the emulation of the B2C / last mile paradigm to continue to enhance and retain the consumer for a more extended period, thereby impacting customer loyalty.

1.5 Looking For B2B Suppliers

it might be more comfortable and cost-effective to do everything yourself in the early days of your small business. As you expand, you would possibly need the assistance of a business-to-business (B2B) vendor or partner to perform tasks such as accounting, distribution, manufacturing, and marketing.

Yet you can't just make a bargain with the first dealer you've ever come across. After all, this corporation can play a role in your business, and you need to be confident that you can entrust it with an asset that is as important as your business. Market News Daily asked industry executives to offer guidance on identifying and sustaining the right B2B relationships.

Factors to weigh whether you come across a prospective vendor through your research or on the recommendation of someone else, you will need to decide whether the organization is suited for your market. Our sources told us to ask the vendors the following questions to gain a better understanding of who you will be dealing with: what kind of experience do you have in our particular industry/sector? Any future small business associate you want will have a strong track record. Depending on what type of provider you're searching for, you're going to want to figure out how much they know about dealing with small business in your area, or how much they know about the specific task for which they are needed.

Do you have new, long-term, strategic B2B relationships, and, if so, what is the average duration of the partnership? Longer-term partnerships reflect a commitment to helping business partners grow rather than just participate in transactional transactions. What's the new load on the client? s acknowledged that an organization with a lot of collaborations in place might have a more transactional emphasis.

[Find out] if they are eligible for your job. It's not uncommon for [some] third-party small business to take all the revenues they can and end up overscheduling. What sort of progress, creativity, or change have you helped other small business partners achieve? If appropriate, recommended that specific details or case reports with prior clients be sought. It will help you understand how this small business works as a partner and incorporates innovations and ways of doing business, or whether it merely offers off-the-lf.

May you connect us as a guide to some of your current or former clients? Sure, you can read online testimonials and reviews, but there's nothing about talking to anyone in your place in this business. Eric, CEO and founder of the Retro Fitness workout chain, you would know as much as you can from the experience of a former and current clientele.

Finding a perfect B2B partner, You think you're about to negotiate a deal? Below are a few more tips for building and sustaining a productive relationship.

Establish and explain your priorities. The first step in forming some form of mutual relationship is to identify the goals explicitly. How are you planning to do by collaborating with this organization, and can a collaboration help both of you?

Partnerships often fail because each party has not clearly understood the core objective of the other. If you don't articulate your aim plainly, how do you trust someone else to help you reach it? there a need to figure out what's important to you before you start talking to suppliers to work out then what importance they offer to consumers, s .

Remember the other side of things. While you need to choose the right vendor or manufacturer to satisfy your needs, it's not just about you: any B2B transaction will help both sides in some way. urged small business owners to take the time to consider the priorities of the other client and how the idea will benefit them.

This helps you to reach them with a win-win strategy. Be prepared to clarify your business plan and goals [also] as it is always believed that each side already understands better than the other side does. Chat to other small business owners. If you are going into your first business relationship, you may not know all the ins and outs of operating with another organization. Speaking to other small business owners in your industry who have had successful B2B transactions will help you manage some of the trickier scenarios that may occur.

The Internet has so much information at your fingertips, but the best work in small business is to keep your foot on the field, Talk to others who know what you're doing, and continue there. As long as you're not [direct] rivals, they can always support you. Seek the correct combination between quality and price. Small business also has limited budgets, and often choices are cost-effective. While the price is still a consideration, in many situations, you get what you pay for, s, so you need to understand the total value of the offer for your small business.

Whether it's a vital item that you're trying to outsource or [you want to] use a small business to build something that gives you a strategic edge, you may not want to get the lowest pricing supplier. When it is a less important service [role], price is more of a concern. Realize where your interest is. Continue to revisit the supply chain. Businesses are not independent small business, but rather dynamic environments, demanding good leadership to hold all directions in the same direction. The development of this harmonious climate, which closely ties vendors, producers, operational plans, predictions, logistics, and the like, can be accomplished. However, small business frequently ignores one of the biggest challenges to success: efficiency.

Organizations [need] to obtain a 'bird's eye' view of production across their entire supply chain and make the required changes to ensure low quality will not affect their end-to-end supply chain. They should have open and frank discussions with their vendors in such a manner that they use data to create an honest debate on their quality-related results and the next steps they will take together to repeat achievements or fix problems. Establish a trust-based partnership. Like in every form of relationship, confidence is necessary for the B2B arrangement to work.

1.6 Value Added To Customers Life

Added value is a useful tool that can be used by small business to attract and retain consumers, raise brand recognition, and distinguish one's position on the market. Don't know where to get started? Below are five ways to generate added value that can be quickly applied in your business strategy today:

 Also, understand the viewpoint of your customers. The art of creating added value starts with the opportunity to view your business through the eyes of your customers.

Think about what is relevant to your target audience and whether your product or service can help you. Which kind of question does it solve, how is it going to help them conquer challenges or make their work better? Most businesses miss the plane by relying on functionality instead of profits.

Through turning your attention to delivering content that reflects on the interests of your clients, you will continue helping and avoid selling.

Creating Consumers helps offer information on your existing and potential clients, what makes them essential, and gives you a blueprint of the type of content you will build and distribute to add value.

Consistently striving to boost consumer service While the argument on whether the consumer is always correct (or not!) persists, lack of customer loyalty is a sure-fire way to prevent customers from coming back. Having accurate reviews by-polls daily helps you to hold your finger on the pulse of your customers 'interests when traveling in your small business and is also an incentive to track the brand's reputation in the marketplace.

Free survey platforms, including Survey Monkey, KwikSurveys, and Survey Planet, provide easy-to-use models and unrestricted responses to ensure that feedback is obtained and an action plan based on findings is created.

Implement marketing models into your strategy As you look for opportunities to generate added value, the use of standard marketing models will help define your strategy. In small to medium-sized business, the Four Cs concept, the Brand Essence Wheel, and the SWOT Analysis method can help you build the brand's value proposition, identify the main selling point, and also forecast consumer needs based on industry dynamics.

Developing excellent customer experience in Small business with outstanding customer interactions are most likely to benefit from word-of-mouth references, favorable user feedback, and higher retention rates.

When you get going, you'll need to understand all the critical points of your market, from initial lead capture to post-purchase contact, and how to best optimize the customer's added value in the process. Creating a consumer service also helps you to build connections with your clients so that you can interact at a degree that goes beyond just making a sale.

More critically, unforgettable consumer engagement models aim to offer the unique intrinsic value that cannot be bundled or marketed. This requires tailored support, attention to detail, and a sense of urgency to resolve issues as they emerge.

Never underestimate the importance of free content, whether it's a downloadable book, a printable PDF, or a small business-branded calendar, free resources are a perfect way to generate added value and highlight the brand's potential to give 'a little extra' to consumers. Free resources can also act as valuable opportunities to help raise the visibility of the brand of small business and to introduce the consumer audience to a range of goods and services.

For brick and mortar locations, find advertising items of the business logo that can be displayed in-store. Businesses with an online presence should use a personalized sign-up page to enable guests to sign up and learn more about promotional deals and promotions.

Note, while you might be providing it for free, it always has to be relevant to your audience, and it should still be aligned with the general intent of your brand.

CHAPTER 2: ADVERTISING AND MARKETING

An advertisement is a form of contact that persuades and inspires people to take concrete action, whether an entrepreneur or a business does the ad. Communication is vital because it keeps people in touch with the many things that the market has to deliver. Announcements often demonstrate the functionality and qualities of the benefits of a single business. The action can be a transaction or a contribution. One of the outcomes of advertising is to change people's commercial behavior.

It is also essential for marketers to interact with consumers. 'Marketing and communication' is a term that demonstrates all the pieces of the marketing cycle of an organization. It includes customer service and analysis. Many businesses conduct communications analysis to consider their customers.

Communication is the process of using signs, symbols, and pictures to communicate meaning to make sense or to share information. Marketing contact includes sharing information about a specific product and service. Publicity is a compelling means of contact. Communication is a routine method of carrying on information from one party to another.

There is a connection between advertisement and marketing since the small-scale enterprise cannot advertise without communicating with its stakeholders. Relationships between the two are in the group the production of communications modes of contact and customer service. When the entrepreneur uses them right, they may affect sales and profits.

2.1 Building a Brand Image

In dynamic markets, products and technologies are compatible and readily replaceable. For a business to stand out, it needs to add value to its brand.

In this period, corporate reputation depends not only on what you offer but also on who you are. Forty-eight percent of customers said they would not partner with a brand they dislike while 37 percent said they would pay some extra amount for a commodity sold by a brand they like. Today's public is fascinated with honesty, which is why small-scale enterprises should be more concerned about credibility than ever before. To create a brand name that is admired, first of all, you need a clear understanding of what your brand stands for a fantastic brand image and personality.

The method of creating a brand is essential and starts with the discovery of meaning.

Is the business in a state of uncertainty over various things? Does your supported adds reflect one thing when the services provided by you are something else altogether? It's time to get your act together. The identity of a business's logo is quite significant. It provides a single picture to the customers.

In an increasingly competitive industry, the identity of a business is more likely to help you draw consumers to your product than other products today because they both know and trust you. No one will ever trust a brand that respects others who show themselves in one way and then turn out to be vague. To create a strong brand reputation for your business work on following tips

Emphasis on Identity Building. Note that any attempt you can make to build a name for your business is only going to be less. But keep in mind that all your advertising needs to be focused on making the benefits more tangible for your customer base. You will attract the viewers with out-of-the-box tactics that need to be addressed.

Create a logo. The easiest way to describe your brand is to construct a logo for your product. Use business colors to create a distinctive illustration and define the police logo. The picture will be the business's id-card to consumers around the world.

Consistent Image Many businesses assume that brand identity can be created by a traditional corporate manual. They're choosing standard layouts business colors and issuing a logo.

Be clear Headed to do this; you need to compare your brand's internal and external perceptions starting with marketer's managers' salespeople and service managers. Compare the view of your customers because where there is a consensus, there would be brand equity. Contradictions are also pleasant because they promote active contact.

Choose the best medium to represent your business. Various mediums can help you accomplish a range of goals. Ads such as video advertising are best designed for creating recognition, not for reacting. Such issues are critical when you agree on your marketing objectives.

Dissolve borders Conventional and social media distinctions must be raised to ensure that marketing practices, including specific brand expenditure roles, are no longer disrupted.

Be Creative Arts and crafts play an essential part in helping the business's brand identity rise. Innovative artwork is not only eye-catching because there are many prospective buyers but also in the case of individual enterprises such as those concerned with architecture enough to demonstrate their abilities. In this new age, you've got precisely 20 seconds to leave an everlasting impact. During this time, show your viewpoint and cultivate your brand. It doesn't matter how good the entrepreneur is working if it doesn't get customers happy. Do an excellent job, man!

Rebrand, if Necessary, this indicates a mistake you've made with your branding before doesn't be afraid to change it back immediately. It's all right to rebrand yourself, particularly if you feel the need to improve the image of your business in the view of potential clients.

Stop Cheap Tricks Don't substitute flashy gimmicks for hard work and contemplation. If your brand name is not where it should be, no amount of eBooks or webinars or SEO will ever be able to save you. Please! Please! Reassess!

2.2 How Much to Be Allocated On Marketing

Marketing is a vital component of every enterprise. To attract consumers and boost sales, you need to work out how to sell your goods and services to your target audience successfully — and this requires a dedicated marketing budget.

With so many different marketing options to explore — from ad campaigns to events — it proves to be tricky to know where to start and how much to spend. That's why a marketing budget is crucial. Not only does it help you focus your approach, but it also makes it easier to keep track of growth and spending goals.

Ready to get going, huh? Take these five measures to set up a marketing budget for your small business.

1. Gather your information you need to develop a marketing plan. Examining the selling process and studying the clients will teach you which marketing strategies are most active.

Do you need some help researching your clients? Check out our comprehensive overview of newbie market research.

Start by evaluating the data from each phase of the selling enclosure — from understanding to practice. Use customer relationship management software such as Hub spot or Sales force or a web analytics tool like Google Analytics to find out visitors business sees per month how many leads you generate and how many points you convert to sales.

Consider the different marketing methods you use to spread awareness, raise interest, and encourage action. How much money and time do you spend on each process, and how active is that channel? Answering these questions will help decide which tactics are stopping or improving your overall progress.

First, get to know the intended market. In addition to researching the existing consumer preferences, do some market research, and figure out the age group place and the average salary of your target customers as well as the brands they gravitate towards.

It is also helpful to understand the habits problems and preferences of your target audience as these factors inform which distribution channels will be most successful.

2. Setting targets goals not just establish a structure for the overall marketing strategy: they often determine the campaign expenditure. When setting goals, take into account your financial experience and potential sales estimates as well as the current stage of your market.

For example, if your business is relatively young, you may need to devote more resources to promotion to gain momentum. While your business is more established and has consistently high revenues, you may be able to scale back to specific strategies.

Regardless of the development stage of your business, you should focus on setting targets that meet the SMART formula — meaning that they should be precise tangible, attainable practical, and time-sensitive.

For example, instead of setting large targets to raise revenue or broaden your client base, set goals to enhance social media participation by a small percentage of increase the number of leads you receive each month from 75 to 100.

3. Organize the finances it is necessary to have an understanding of the gross margins and operational expenses and decide how much money you should reasonably invest in ads. Start by listing the various business expenses, including fixed and variable costs. Fixed payments include recurring expenditures such as leases salaries and insurance. In contrast, discretionary expenses include investments that fluctuate from month to month, such as office supplies services and repair of facilities.

For businesses selling merchandise, the next move is to decide the cost of goods sold (COGS) or the amount of money required to produce and market the items. It covers raw materials as well as packing delivery and storage charges.

To measure how much it takes to produce and deliver the goods using the following formula: COGS = Early Year Production Cost + Additional Year Bought Production Cost – End of Year Inventory Cost From these simple calculations one can determine how much money they earn:

Net Income = Sales – COGS – Expenditures Net Profit Margin = Net Profit / Total Revenue x

10. Small Business Administration suggests that small-scale enterprises spend 7-8% of their total sales on ads suggesting that they receive less than $5 million in revenue and have a net margin of between 10% and 12%.

Well, that said, every business is different. How much you spend on ads depends on various variables such as your business, your competition, your priorities, your financial condition, and your internal capacity to handle production.

4. Determine your channel. The delivery strategies you select fall into one of two categories: inbound or outbound marketing.

Inbound marketing is intended to introduce prospective clients to you. It involves costs associated with managing a website optimizing SEO operating a blog or other content promotion or creating a personalized chart video or case study that supports your brand.

Know how to bring more leads to your business through content marketing.

Outbound marketing refers to any approach that lets you distribute your advertisement or product to prospective customers. This can take the form of publicity campaign banners, promotional materials, or activities.

Compile a list of all your inbound and outbound campaign plans and then sum up the expenses of those to see if they fit under your current budget. If not, you may need to reassess your plans or change your spending.

According to the survey, in 2018, entrepreneurs spent 29 percent of their marketing budget on marketing technology such as digital analytics platforms and web content management. Other specific spending areas include ads that account for over 21 percent of marketing budgets and internet services such as paid search and organic search, which make up 25 percent of budgets.

If your marketing budget is not big enough to cover every region give priority to the methods most likely to produce the highest returns for your business. You should also concentrate on low-cost high-impact approaches such as email marketing and social media.

5. Keep checking and modifying is not a one-time operation. When you know more about your clients and play with new marketing tactics, your campaign strategy will evolve — which means that your budget will likely shift.

This is a smart idea to track and review your campaign activities and ensure that you attract as many consumers as possible in a cost-effective manner. At least once a fifth set aside time to analyze what does what doesn't and why.

Use some of these tools to check and track the efficacy of your marketing efforts:

- Google Analytics: Monitor traffic to your business page where the traffic originates and analyze the effectiveness of your marketing campaigns
- A / B optimization apps: Use a platform like Optimize, you can check A / B text photos and more and see what works best for your marketing strategies.
- In-suite email marketing services: using a tool like Mail Chimp or Campaign Control, you can send targeted emails to see how they function.
- Social Media Marketing Software: As most social sites offer their analytics resources (think Facebook Analysis for Business Pages); you can also use third-party apps like Hoot suite or Sprout Social to manage your social activity and campaigns in one location.

From there, recommend eliminating or rising spending on tactics that display little to no ROI while dedicating more money to the most effective channels. Bear in mind that the right campaign strategy is one that expands with the business rather than locking you in.

6. Developing a marketing budget for your business might sound overwhelming; however, it doesn't have to be challenging. Work on outlining a campaign plan first and start to mess around with the figures and delivery strategies until you figure out what works.

2.3 Making the Sales

Everything occurs before the transaction has taken place. Salespeople are two of the most influential people in our culture. No profits our whole business should have come to a grinding halt.

Businesses are the only real producers of riches in our culture. By generating both goods and services, they are making both profits and property. Businesses are also paying for wages and benefits.

You are the most valuable salespeople in any sector. Without profits, the most important and most innovative businesses will be shut down. Sales are a spark plug in a free market engine. There is a clear relationship between the success of the business sector and the prosperity of the country as a whole. The more unusual the amount of revenue, the more competitive and prosperous the business or the region would be.

Sales associates — through their revenues and income and taxes generated by profitable small-scale enterprise — pay for policy at all rates, including all healthcare health compensation social security Medicare and other services. By following the principle discussed, we will increase our profits to an impressive amount. The 80/20 law, also referred to as the Pareto Principle, is credited to the Italian economist Wilfred Pareto. In one of hiss, Pareto noted that about 80 percent of the land in Italy belonged to about 20 percent of the country's total population. Necessarily the Pareto Theory infers that there is an 80-to-20 relationship between the consequences and their sources.

The Pareto Theory transcends specialization. For athletics, for example, you can note that at least 20 percent of athletes compete for 80 percent of the time or that about 20 percent of preparation and practice influences 80 percent of an athlete's success. Likewise, as far as treatment is concerned, about 20% of patients rely on as much as 80% of the nation's healthcare services.

Applying it to the corporate world, the 80/20 concept implies that 80% of the business's revenues come from 20% of your clients. Alternatively, you could say that 20% of what you do is 80% of the outcome of that particular activity.

Understanding the dilemma for your customers is probably the most significant obstacle you can face when you start a business. Customers need what you sell, and your product needs to solve a real problem. But ensuring the business meets consumer demands is just one aspect of launching a successful business. The other main ingredient is how you're going to make money. That's where the business model fits in.

What's your business model?

Your business model is a definition of how the business earns profits. It describes how you offer value to your customers at an acceptable rate.

According to Joan Magritte in Why Business Models Matter, the term business model became commonly used with the introduction of personal computers and tablets.

Such methods allow entrepreneurs to explore the study and develop various ways to organize their expenses and revenue streams. Spreadsheets help entrepreneurs make fast conceptual adjustments to their business model and see instantly how the change will impact their business now and in the future.

Business structures can be divided into **three parts** in their primary forms:

1. To make something: construction raw materials processing labor etc.

2. What it takes to sell it: marketing distribution service delivery and inventory management.

3. Where and what the consumer pays: sales policy payment forms pacing etc.

If you can see a business model is an analysis of what prices and expenditures you have to spend on a product or service.

A good business model needs to raise more revenue from consumers than what the product expensive. That's your profit — simple. You can lower costs during design and manufacturing, or you may consider more successful marketing and selling methods.

Yet note you don't have to come up with a different marketing idea to create a successful approach. Instead, you may take a proven business model and sell it to different customers. For example, restaurants run more on a traditional business model but concentrate their approach on attracting specific customer groups.

You don't have to create a whole new business model for beginning a business. In reality, the vast majority of small-scale enterprises use proven business models to gain a competitive advantage.

Here's a list of business models to launch your own business.

1. Advertisement, The advertising industry model has been around for a long time and got more complex as the market moved from print to online. Model basics are about producing content that people choose to read or watch and then showing ads to the readers or audiences.

In an advertisement market model, two target segments must be satisfied: the listeners or audiences and marketers. Your viewers may or may not pay you; however, your advertisers do.

Often an advertisement business model is paired with a crowdsourcing approach where you get your content free from consumers instead of charging web owners to create it.

2. The franchise, the franchise business model, is similar to the advertisement business model, which with some variations. More commonly found online, the partnering paradigm uses content-embedded connections instead of readily recognizable display advertising.

For example, if you have a book review website, you might have promotional links to Amazon in your reviews to encourage users to purchase the book you review. Amazon will give you a small fee on any sale you make.

3. Brokerage small-scale enterprise binds buyers and sellers to promote trade. They bill the buyer or seller for each sale and sometimes both.

One of the more popular brokerage small-scale enterprises is a real estate service. Still, there are several other forms of brokerage such as freight brokers and brokers who aid construction firms locate dirt buyers they excavate from new foundations.

4. Personalized aspects, many small-scale enterprises take current goods or services and add a personalized aspect to the deal that makes each sale exclusive to the buyer.

Remember, for example, specialty travel agents scheduling journeys and events for wealthy customers. You will also expect individuality on a broader scale for items like Nike's custom shoes.

5. Crowdsourcing If you can get a vast amount of people together to add material to your platform, you're crowdsourcing. Crowdsourcing market models are often combined with advertisement models to raise sales, although there are also such model variations. For example, thread less lets designers upload t-shirt designs giving designers a percentage of sales.

Small-scale enterprises seeking to solve severe problems also freely post their challenges for others to try to fix. Successful approaches are compensated, and business will then expand. The trick to a profitable crowdsourcing business has the right incentives to draw the crowd while helping you to develop a sustainable business.

Getting more appointments selling by the numbers

Sales executives realize that they're playing a game of numbers: the more opportunities you have and the more ideas you submit, the more deals you're going to close next year.

Each step in the selling cycle is equally critical and is faced with unexpected challenges. Finding a buyer convincing them to open up to you selling the offer and closing the deal can all be hard work. Once you hit the street and start trading, you need to consider the four phases that most sales processes have in common:

1. Prospecting for Clients

Prospecting is when the selling process begins. It includes finding future buyers who might benefit from the commodity you're offering. A big part of prospecting is not only finding prospective buyers but also checking on them to make sure they are in the right position. You can do so by making a cold or warm phone call delivering direct mail with personalized surveys, or make a face-to-face meeting so you can learn more about your future client.

2. Having an appointment

After you have established and approached your opportunities, the next move is to get a date. When a candidate has answered your call, you've got about 10 to 20 seconds to catch their eye and make your pitch. If you practice your strategy beforehand, you would have a better chance of keeping them on the track. Make sure you do your homework so that you know precisely how your business will help. Having an appointment with your prospect is usually an indication of desire, and any meeting can be seen as a success.

3. Submitting a proposal

If the consultation goes well, you will be asked to send a project to your prospective client detailing the proposed solution along with the price timeline and other applicable warranty details. Being quick increase the offers you will make to interested people the more sales you can ultimately generate.

4. Closing the Contract

Every step in the buying process leads to the closure of the transaction. When you have done an excellent job of identifying customers who need your product or service and an equally meticulous job of developing a project that meets their needs otherwise you will both be prepared to receive a fee. This sounds much simpler than it is, of course, so it's much more complicated if you haven't done an excellent job of prospecting setting up a meeting and presenting a presentation to each prospective customer.

How to Set up and play the Business Numbers Game

You need to start knowing the expectations to pay package to decide how much money you expect to gain to be satisfied in your new work. When you've made up your mind, find out how much you're making on regular sales — or if you're fresh to your position — ask your bosses what you would hope to gain for each transaction.

Divide the overall targeted revenue by the fee from the average sale; the effect would be the number of transactions you need to close in one year to meet the revenue goal.

First, assess how many ideas submitted end in a closed deal. If you intend to make 50 sales to meet your goal and believe that you will need to make five proposals to close one contract, it follows that you will need to make 250 proposals a year to make 50 sales.

The next step is to decide how many meetings you need to make before reaching a client who is willing (and qualified) to submit a request. Assume that you require two appointments to lock in the future; as such, you will need to set up 500 meetings each year to complete 250 proposals effectively.

The last move is to figure out how many prospecting calls (cold calls hot calls emails, etc.) you need to make to have one meeting.

Adding the percentages together Assume that you intend to make five calls to schedule one meeting two appointments to schedule one request and five proposals to reach one arrangement. If you've got your cumulative amount of purchases (to meet your revenue goal), work backward to get the actual figures.

For the example above, you will need 1500 prospecting calls to secure 500 meetings, which will yield 250 offers resulting in 50 deals being closed.

You're going to need to calculate your figures for this exercise to be successful, so if you know the numbers, you will approach your days with a much stronger emphasis. If you end up having to make 1500 prospecting calls a year, you can reduce this amount to annual weekly and daily operation levels. If you work 250 days a year and your numbers show you need to make 1500 prospecting calls during that time, you will have a regular target of six bells.

By conceptualizing your sales goal as a number game, you can turn methodical day-to-day action into a more productive way of prospecting and closing new customers.

E-commerce and sales automation

At its heart, e-commerce is purchasing and selling online goods and services. However, the word also defines all the actions of a seller in the purchase process. This begins when a potential customer hears about a product and wants to purchase use and hopefully continuing consumer loyalty. Data power the most effective e-commerce operations using best practices such as targeted email marketing customer segmentation and marketing automation.

E-commerce is work with enormous obligations. Especially in the current scenario of intense competition from domestic and foreign brands, you cannot expect to stand out without adjusting to new trends and strategic ecommerce solutions.

E-Commerce Automation's approach. Even as a one-person army, you can't run your business manually. And if you did on any field, you'd still find yourself lagging behind your rivals.

If not all, then at least some aspects of your operation deserve automation to keep things smooth and competitive, mainly as your business grows significant with time. In this post, we will enlist five such e-commerce marketing automation hacks that you can implement in your business and win sales way better than your competitors.

Automation can seem like a deep word requiring massive AI investments and costly custom innovations. Yet automation isn't just about expensive solutions. Whether you are working in an inventory model or a multivendor marketplace model, you can follow multiple small and inexpensive automation techniques to streamline a variety of complicated tasks with simple button clicks:

- You can eliminate human errors from repetitive tasks
- You can optimize your business for expansion

- With easy automation, you can improve your ecommerce marketing plan, shipping infrastructure conversion optimization techniques, and more.

    1. Automating your welcome notes

Welcoming new customers with a warm message looks like a trivia. Not many entrepreneurs, however, realize this could be the first step towards acquiring a loyal customer and building trust in your business. It looks like nothing but shockingly with a welcoming message; only 75% of online stores greet their new customer and newly registered users. It's because sending welcome notes is routine, usually involving manual labor.

Do you know that welcome emails provide 400 percent stronger commitments than any other kind of email you will ever give to your prospects? It's time to automate your welcome notes and use the opportunity to attract happier customers to promote your brand and create confidence. You can customize your email notes from any good ecommerce site you are using with simple SMTP settings. Here's a screenshot from the Magneto back-end app to set up your SMTP email with straightforward measures.

All other popular ecommerce sites have similar settings to automate your emails. Yes, several of these platforms can also streamline various welcome email templates. If not present, you can install a custom module plugin or extension to get this feature; it's not expensive.

More interestingly, you can add another channel to this automation with web push notifications. You may also start sending welcome push notifications to your customers and new users. The best part is to push notification needs no specific customer or device information. By clicking the Allow button of a push alerts subscription dialog box, users consent to accept push notifications from your website.

You can send any number of push notifications to these users whenever you wish. Mind this device because we will explore further how to automate several other items with push notifications.

2. Automating your drip campaigns

Once you sort your welcome plan with email and push notifications, it's time to order your long-term contact channel with your customers. Drip campaigns are all about streamlining the website's smooth conversion funnel, enabling a newly joining user actually to become a customer, and keep coming back. We're talking about small-automation upgrading the conversion funnel.

The same email and push tools we used for phase one can also help you create smart drip campaigns. You can set different email moves and even SMS models to stay in contact with prospects at various levels.

- Day 1: Give a welcome message
- Day 2: Send new users an exclusive bid. Club this with a welcome message too.
- Day 8: Submit another proposal or update on new stock product suggestions etc. Send a gentle reminder with some FOMO features, such as limited time if not converted.
- Days 15: It's time to communicate with customers. You can submit ideas links or something that doesn't sound like a sales pitch. You may also invite me to join you on social media in surveys or contests.
- Day 20: Send new offers and deals based on past purchasing history. Encourage more shopping.

Start with email move and SMS campaigns. Several email SMS and push automation tools you can use to build drip campaigns are Mail Chimp Hub Spot Twilit iota etc.

3. Automating Social Media

FOMO promotions are the perfect way to make FOMO for the prospects. This is where the latest product's current deals and what everybody else is buying these days keep updated. You can use your customers to inspire others to purchase via simple FOMO automation through social media.

Encourage your consumers to join you on social media tag you on posts and exchange sales and promotions. You may use specific motivating points such as special offers or an exclusive membership package and activities. When others see these people engaged with your business, they'd probably be interested in learning what's going on. You may use various social media platforms to simplify the whole process. For example:

- A tool to plan your social media messages
- A tool to watch your brand's social media mentions
- A tool to get your social media updates to your website
- Social networking advertising re-targeting apps and resources

Examples of apps you may use include Schedule Hub spot FOMO Buffer BuzzSumo Hoot suite etc. Referral and loyalty marketing services have been an essential aspect of every ecommerce marketing plan these days. If you run a small online store, these two elements are required to draw prospects.

By offering referrers and referred consumers to some advantages, you should hope to gain fast attention due to the massive impact of mouth marketing on online shoppers these days. Users can re-offer other users to enter your store or purchase a product and receive exclusive discount coupons or affiliate commissions.

Luckily several ecommerce sites have built-in discount voucher service loyalty marketing and referral services. Many that lack such features, however, can add other plugins and enhancements to gain such features.

5. Automating your abandoned cart recovery, Small web stores, and huge multivendor marketplace are now a reality.

Sites can't stop dumping carts. With certain UX optimization methods, you can that them to an extent, but some abandonments are paramount. Therefore you shouldn't avoid improving your market but also build a parallel abandoned cart recovery strategy.

One such tactic is to build automatic email and push programs to give subtle alerts to consumers leaving shopping carts. There are two ways to make these campaigns, so you will use them for improved results: email: you should use your ecommerce platform's shopping cart recovery tool or extension to manage the lost carts. These applications can catch the email address of customers who install items in their carts but don't complete the order. The package can create a new consumer email list in your account, which you can combine with your email marketing platform to create an email drip plan.

Push update: There are industry push update platforms and utilities with built-in abandoned cart monitoring systems. Using set templates, you can program these tools to track and submit automatic push notifications. You can create a drip pan and set various push models at different points of the cart recovery process.

In any case, you will build some models and adjust settings to plan your program. You can configure the software to use other coupon codes alert spacing message size and specific behavior-based section users. Strategic use of these devices will simplify your abandoned cart recovery and help you win back your conversions without manual labor. If you want to remain competitive on the market, that's the type of ecommerce automation you should aim for today.

No lack of ways to acquire valuable ecommerce automation for your business. Let's not mention AI catboats. Though pricey, they have proven to be one of the most significant automation devices in not just ecommerce but any other domain. Besides, certain pop-ups can also be automated on your web. You can cause pop-ups newsletter delivery pop-ups stock alert and many more.

In short, AI catboats and virtual assistants may be the leading automation tools for business process management, but they are not readily available to small businesses. That doesn't mean you can't simplify your marketing campaign and many other facets without costing a lot. There are forms to do it, and we've seen it in this post.

Pros and cons advantages for appropriate structure owning a small business has its advantages and its disadvantages. Every entrepreneur must weigh the pros and cons carefully and decide whether or not the risk is worth the reward.

Advantages of Small Business Ownership

- Equality. Equality. Entrepreneurs became their own managers. They make choices and make decisions. You chose for whom you will do business and what job you will do. We determine what hours to work and when to take a break. Most businessmen have ample flexibility to monitor their fortunes to resolve possible risks.
- Economic gains. Entrepreneurship provides more incentives to gain significant financial rewards than to work with someone else. The control of your own business reduces the revenue limitation when someone else works. Many businessmen are motivated by the tremendous

millionaires we have today, for example, Steve Jobs Leon Musk Jeff Bezos and Mark Zuckerberg.

- Control, please. It enables one to participate in the overall operation of the business from concept to design creation from sales to marketing and customer response. This ability to be immersed in business is very satisfying for entrepreneurs who are driven by passion and creativity and who have a vision of what they want to achieve. This level of involvement allows the owner of the business to create something of his own.

- Prestige, please. It offers the status of being in charge. Some entrepreneurs are attracted to the idea that they are the boss. Also, however, there is prestige and pride of ownership. When someone asks, who did it? The entrepreneur can answer I did it.

- Equity. It allows an individual to build equity that can be maintained sold or passed on to the next generation. It's not unusual for entrepreneurs to own multiple businesses throughout their lives. They set up a business run it for a while and then sell it to someone else. The revenue from this sale can then be used to finance the next venture. If they are not interested in selling a business, the goal may be to build something which can become their legacy, which will help ensure their financial future. One thing is sure: to fully reap the economic benefits of a business venture, you need to be the owner.

- Possibility. Entrepreneurship provides an opportunity for a person to contribute. Most new entrepreneurs are helping the local economy. Some — through their innovations — contribute to society as a whole.

    Small businesses do have other benefits over big corporations. Small businesses typically focus on versatility and their ability to establish close consumer relationships. The revolution in modern media has considerably cut retail prices and become a boon for new start-ups and big business alike.

Small Business Ownership Disadvantages

There are some pitfalls for a small business: time commitment. When anyone sets up a small business, at least they will have few employees at the outset. This leaves the owner with both responsibilities and tasks. Small business owners are operating for 80 hours a week, from sales to banking and advertising. Such dedication will place pressure on family and friends and contribute to the tension of beginning a new business.

- Danger. However, if the organization is designed to mitigate damage and owner responsibility, the damage cannot be excluded. For example, if someone leaves a stable job for an ambitious vision and the business fails, it becomes impossible to solve this financial setback. In addition to financial risks, product liability concerns and compliance standards are not taken into account by businesses. Uncertainty. While the business is initially competitive, external factors such as economic downturns may hamper new competitors entering the market or changes in customer demand. Yet businessmen who follow a rigorous preparation phase will never foresee future market shifts.

- Economic contribution. This personal contribution. Also, the smallest businesses require some money to start up. The primary source of financing for other start-ups is financial investments or retirement funds. The gift of these funds to a corporation will not make them eligible for employee or family requirements. Where a small business earns start-up financing via a loan, an entrepreneur can protect the loan by making personal properties such as a house available. Economic wealth at home is not just businessmen ready to make a financial investment. Given the possible pitfalls, most small business owners are happy to start their business.

Payment procedures

It's just good business offering your customers payment options. These options may include payment plans using credit or debit card online payments checks cash orders cashier checks automatic or western withdrawals.

People appear to resist what they are being imposed. Citizens prefer to embrace what they do. I'm sure you can link your customers to this line. When you contact a prior due customer and demand full payment, you do not hit the stage where you contact to provide multiple payment processing solutions.

You are giving suggestions for realistic consumer payment plans if you have never set up payment systems until you get them. One thing you have to do is make sure the client understands you realize that any case is different and the willingness to compensate the outstanding balance for their previous purchase background and the reasons that their bill has been charged in creating a payment plan is taken into account.

Be sure that clients know that you can not necessarily build these payment plans; you do it now when there is a problem, and you want to address it. Consumers also feel very confident to order additional items or services and to pay the monthly payment schedule. You avoid this by writing each document with a beginning and finishing date.

Many businesses have payment systems laws. This may involve not accessing one customer's payment plans more than once a year or having a 15% deposit on all new payment plans.

With the economy, a mess, and more customers struggling to pay their bills, the aim of setting up payment deals is to get something paid rather than nothing. Some consumers look at all their bills and then determine which ones should be charged that month based on what's most important to them. It's your responsibility to make the invoice valuable to them, giving them reasonable choices so they'll pay it every month. You want to detail policies and procedures that will help provide options for your customers when they cannot ultimately pay. Know that if you don't like giving payment plans. When someone owes you money, they presumably owe money to someone, and whoever takes action first or proposes a solution is paid first.

Setting up your payment agreement:

- Check customer history before calling
- Until calling
- Three find two or three payment agreement options. Repeat all for customer
- Get it written and have your customer sign it
- To keep up with the costs of operating a business, all small business owners rely on their customers paying. When payments routinely arrive late, a business may face financial difficulties.

Various negative consequences can affect small businesses as a result of late customer payments which, according to an Entrepreneur post could include:

- Small business owners may no longer pay themselves a wage.
- Some small-scale enterprises cannot invest in the required equipment.
- Several small businesses reduced their marketing budgets, damaging their ability to draw new customers.

The good news is you can take action to make your customers pay more effectively. One such move is to make it easy for customers to pay you by enrolling in an online payment program.

Amazon Payments is a fast online payment-friendly alternative. The app seamlessly blends into the current website enabling consumers to pay for a range of digital products and services instantly.

It's also a seamless approach from the customer's viewpoint as they can pay you directly using the payment details saved in their Amazon.com accounts.

PayPal is also a top-rated online payment service that has supported over 17 million small-scale enterprises with payments and credit solutions. PayPal helps small business owners to accept payments online without a current merchant account.

You can accept credit cards online or by phone via PayPal business services. You can also create and monitor invoices through your PayPal account, so you're paid faster.

For the small-scale retail enterprise, you can accept card payments from your customers in person and process them through PayPal. Download their app and buy a card reader.

2.4 Crypto Currencies Getting Entrepreneurs to the Next Level

The meteoric increase in internet popularity has resulted in the emergence of innovative market ideas that have transformed the game entirely. In addition, this led to a revolution in what it meant to be a businessman. It completely changed the ways in which a business works and compelled business owners to revisit their goals and benchmarks by dramatically changing priorities.

This is somewhat close to the latest market system of the emerging global world. While the block chain model has been used for decades, crypto currencies are at an early point. During this time, the emphasis has also been on short-term gains, such as investing in crypto currencies and trading opportunities. It is necessary for a businessman to understand the central principle of block chain and the seemingly infinite possibilities it provides to completely capitalize on the crypto currency surge.

Block chain technology gives developers a new generation of possibilities in all sectors. You may be an architect, a writer, or a model – you can only carry your idea to your market and enjoy the true rewards of your work.

For an entrepreneur accustomed to working in a mainstream finance environment, attempting to grasp all the excitement around crypto currency can be a struggle to come to terms with the simple understanding of what long-term advantages you have. It doesn't help if you have a sea of self-proclaimed crypto-experts doing whatever you can to grab your attention and position your business on each site. The experienced entrepreneur would take his time to assess the reality of fiction and to bring attention to the crucial facts that will have a significant effect on the way a business is run.

Here's a look at how crypto currency and block chain technology can help you take your business to the next level.

The initial investment to start up a corporation is potentially one of the steepest steps. It is hard to attract customers who are persuaded of your idea, and even though you eventually persuade them in most situations, you are a fool, and your business can not fulfill its success, as it is not what you want to be. This is a terrible waste of money from a specific viewpoint. This is almost natural to accept that as a result of exposure to finance, some of the more important investment innovations will never be adopted.

If you take the scenario of an economy run by the first coin offering of block chain technology, it's the default move to establishing a business. Because block chain is decentralized, no string pulls intermediaries in order to benefit from absolute openness and maximum performance.

ICO's benefit is that the business's appraisal is completed nearly instantly. You get a huge amount of equity for your business with tokens as shares.

When you hold your hands to the table, more and more small businesses will declare their date and set up new and creative ventures. What is interesting about the ICO is that it does not conform to today's industry laws. Anyone can browse coin deals anywhere in the world. This ensures that you meet a far larger market and, therefore, an incredibly knowledgeable investor base. The ICO-driven economy works with speed and flexibility as it reduces the traditional bottlenecks in modern risk capital economies.

You must always realize, as an entrepreneur, that, in the present situation where there is no oversight investing in a coin offering is not inherently always a smart idea. Wherever there is a chance of something so enticing, you should get your share of scammers to prey on the general knowledge lack.

The existence of those intermediaries that build this concentrated influence vacuum is one of the most detrimental facets of today's traditional processes in the market, such as the insurance sector, governance, employment, or even the entertainment industry. You see them on the surface in order to make it simpler as contractors or brokers or regulators. The reality is that such SMEs have a huge deal of power to exploit the system.

You will negotiate with a significant number of such power players if you are operating a business on an international scale. Data from different manufacturing sectors reinforces the idea that these mediums will destroy competition and development force prices up or down control volumes or even get the business off the ground if it meets its objectives.

Crypto currency provides the best option for the removal of these technological bottlenecks through Ethereum's intelligent contract concept.

Smart contracts are completely unaware of any human involvement since they are built on an algorithm. The algorithm tests and authenticates a sequence of transactions automatically.

Anyone participating in this transaction chain will test its validity in this manner.

In theory, this gives businessmen the ability to carry out foreign deals without having to rely on intermediaries to save money and time. What is remarkable is that a knowledgeable contractor can use the brilliant contractual principle to address a range of financial and even environmental logistics issues.

This is perhaps the most significant change for anyone with an entrepreneurial mind to invest early in small businesses with strong growth potential. Personal seed investors and venture capital firms have unique leverage to invest in the world's most highly skilled SMEs. Crypto currency gives the average citizen the capacity to own small SMEs with tremendous potential for growth.

You have access to some of the most creative technological geniuses in the world when you belong to the block chain network. The simplicity and pace at which multimillion-dollar transactions are carried out were remarkable.

We saw communities engage in popular messaging apps like What Sapp We Chat and Facebook to connect every day. Such meek What Sapp communities have made a substantial investment in technology start-ups in a matter of minutes or just seconds. This could take months to execute in traditional environments with regular venture capital.

The idea of crypto currency reflects and reinforces the optimal symbiosis between thought and practice. When you have a bankable idea, you will use the crypto currency network to easily execute it effectively and at dramatically reduced costs. You have access to the most qualified investment-savvy developers and the latest technological tools as members of the block chain network. Such connections are the foundation blocks of your long-term success as an entrepreneur.

A real entrepreneur's long-term aim is not to make productive acquisitions or create big businesses that have a constant stream of income. Therefore, the global effect is to drive progress and update the rules of the game to help everyone. Crypto currency and block chain technologies give you a forum for this.

CHAPTER 3: Environmental Impact of the Business

The location you work will have a substantial positive or negative effect on the environment. The environment of your workplace when it comes to heating and cooling the house, taking goods into it, and extracting waste from it has a significant impact on your society and the world. Some of the concrete examples of how modern life is destroying the environment are:

- Carbon gas pollutants from workplaces into the soil are emitted by heating, and air conditioning equipment and vast quantities of energy are used. Many buildings are not built to incorporate energy-efficient heating and air-conditioning systems and technology.

- Most structures are constructed of non-renewable materials material.

- Office buildings have a high demand for lighting power, air conditioning, monitors, printers, and photocopiers. Equipment can be left 24 hours a day, seven days a week — even though nobody works.

- Offices consume large amounts of paper. Even with more paper recycling offices, a large number of paper wastes still go to landfills or incinerators.

- In addition to writing, offices produce a lot of other debris, including equipment (especially computers), because small business-enterprise regularly upgrade their equipment to remain competitive. Electronics, such as photocopiers and machines, can end up in landfills where they do not break down and, worse still, can leave harmful chemicals in the soil and water.

- Rush-hour queues in towns and villages are full of people rushing to get to work — time lost and the air poisoned.

The United States of America says. The agricultural and commercial energy usage (from electrical uses, transportation of goods, manufacturing processes, boiler fossil fuel combustion and steam generation, and the gasoline used in powered vehicles) accounts for about 30 percent of overall U.S. greenhouse gas emissions.

Importance of Eco-friendly Goods Everybody needs to give their families the best; if it means the best Diet or health services of the most exceptional quality, any parent or guardian wishes to give their children the best of the best. While looking at family items, it is vital to understand all the results of the items used. Many of this small business-enterprise are sneaky and can use harmful or even dangerous chemicals to make their goods as inexpensive as possible, totally disregarding the protection and health of customers.

Several consumers have investigated and selected for harmful goods and have preferred to choose environmentally friendly products that help both the environment and their communities. Not understanding what goes into a product that a family uses daily may be of concern to many households, particularly those with children. Some are already worrying that they are only purchasing eco-friendly goods, so what are these goods, and why are they the better option?

This term specifically applies to a substance that is not toxic to the environment. Though it can be more complicated than that because many reasons may be "harmful to the atmosphere." Too many other items can harm the environment, such as not following appropriate protocols when disposing of goods. Nevertheless, there are other advantages of the use of eco-friendly products that are not only based on the safety and well-being of the Planet, but rather on the safety and well-being of your children.

While many businesses and their goods claim to be environmentally friendly, they can misconstruction their facts, leaving customers puzzled and sometimes blindly purchasing their products. When looking for eco-friendly items, search for

- Energy Star – for energy-saving devices and equipment
- USDA Organic Seal – for sustainable cosmetics and food
- Green Seal – for environmentally responsible cleaning goods

If you don't see these seals or logos on the goods, a decent sign is accessible. To stop inadvertently purchasing goods that are unsafe to both families and the Planet, look for these seals of approval and be assured of protection!

Eco-friendly goods that appear to be more costly, but they are often more cost-effective in the long run. Eco-friendly goods tend to last longer. Such products are usually made from recycled materials and are sturdy, resistant to any drops, falls, and dishwashers. Eco-friendly goods can have a higher retail price, but because they last longer, it is an expense that will pay off.

In addition to the eco-friendly advantages, there are also specific advantages that align with the use of all-natural goods. Plastics, for example, are known to contain BPA, asbestos, and other toxic contaminants that can cause many different infections and illnesses in both children and adults. Risks for adults include diabetes, heart disease, infectious disease, and reproductive system disorders. This may induce early puberty, diabetes, stunted development, and autoimmune disorders in infants. Eco-friendly, all-natural goods guarantee the health of all dangerous substances and encourage families to prevent harmful ingredients that might cause either of these problems. The use of eco-friendly products increases the quality of life in terms of death, sex, cancer, and illness. We guarantee the health of families and the world.

There are several different kinds of eco-friendly goods available. That of them guarantees a reliable commodity that helps both the consumers and the world.

Reusable Coffee Cups: We all get a warm cup of Joe in the morning, alas, it also means that every morning we have a new plastic cup (and generally a lid, too!). For those on-the-go go, having a reusable container of coffee may be the difference, not only how much packaging is being used, but how much money is being spent in these cups. The benefits are significant for both the pocket and the climate.

Recycled Toilet Paper: It isn't as weird as it sounds. Recycled toilet paper is a perfect substitute for actually buying non-organic toilet paper. It's typically cheaper than the standard version, so it's available from most retailers. Especially if there is a young adult who likes to use a bit too much toilet paper, it's an excellent idea to contribute back to the world.

Reusable Bags: We've all used super-market plastic bags to fill our small garbage cans or put them in our vehicles to catch odd straw wrappers. There are—however, other options to re-use plastic bags. Most businesses sell recycled plastic items, such as reusable lunch bags, grocery bags, and recycled garbage bags.

Cleaning Products: Many of the most important ways to spend in "going green" are in the cleaning department. Harsh chemicals such as ammonia, antibacterial soap, and multi-purpose cleaners are all dangerous items to be used inside and outside the house. These contaminants are not only harmful to the environment, but they are also bad for people at home since most of them are poisonous or may induce disease or sickness. There are plenty of safer, healthier, cleaner choices, such as the use of probiotic cleaners that are environmentally friendly and non-risky. These items will make your home clean without removing the healthy bacteria that hang around to support the family's immunity!

Eco-Friendly Technology: gadgets make up most of our lives at this time and era. Through televisions to mobile phones, our lives are about electronics. But, these devices require charging, which requires a lot of energy and can increase the power bill, or use batteries that can be almost as bad. Such radical goods damage our world (and your wallet!). Instead, switch to eco-friendly electronics, such as low-light computers and televisions, which do not glow brightly but can have an outstanding image and color. Another choice is to change the light bulbs for low-watt bulbs or to change them to eco-friendly bulbs in general. All this is going to help both the family and our world.

Overall, these items are state-of-the-artist, innovative, and always save you money and encourage you to escape wastefulness, but they're more than just right for you. The earth needs our support in today's climate. Our abuse of wealth has placed the world in a difficult situation, and we are the only ones who can avoid destruction. While it can be impossible to make a big difference as a single person, the recycling of resources and the use of eco-friendly goods is a beautiful way for each citizen to engage in the protection of our earth and environment.

Through using environmentally friendly goods, each individual contributes to the health and protection of the Planet's resources, such as metals, plastics, and even water. As more consumers are using eco-friendly goods, the cost of such products will decrease, and all humans, both human and animal, will benefit.

To maintain the biodiversity, energy, and habitability of the earth, it is crucial that our daily choices have a positive effect on the world. That's where eco-friendly items come in. They are both excellent for families and good for the world, and eco-friendly goods give customers the ability to prioritize duty over frivolity. Eco-friendly products are both healthy for the environment and safe for customers! They're an excellent choice for families everywhere.

3.1 Go Green with Your Business

The 'carbon' sector aims to impact the environment and the culture favorably. Develop and practice business strategies to go beyond regulation and demonstrate a commitment to a safe, balanced future.

Environmentalism is rising over, and you are looking for an increasing market. The German-speaking Roland Berger Strategy Consultants reports that by 2020 the total value of "environmental innovations" on the market is projected to hit $2,740 billion.

You should be especially pleased with beginning a green business as you lead to a healthier position in the world.

Help green business grow. The growing question about the source of food and what has been achieved is being reflected in a rising number of people who want to cultivate food everywhere they stay. Gardens for small areas Small-scale planting concepts can be created for businesses in many ways:

- Produce garden sets, low ranges of planted plant tables suitable on the modest balcony, enabling people to cultivate their vegetables.
- As a landscape designer, you might specialize in roof landscape projects on a broader scale.
- Establish a green business focused on goods that help people grow their food, such as housing friendly

greenhouses or biological pest control. The National Gardening Association's 2014 report revealed that one household in three in the US cultivates their vegetables, nuts, berries, or herbs.

- Worm cultivation and the selling of organic manure are two ecological farming concepts that might work for you.

Help them to reduce their prices of electricity. Solar power generation and solar water heating systems Conventional electricity prices tend to raise green business concepts for energy efficiency and utility expense reductions – a good bet for now and in the future.

Solar water heating systems can provide substantial energy savings (providing, according to some retailers, up to 70% of hot water in the household when correctly installed).

According to the Solar Power Industries Association, between 2006 and 2016, U.S. solar-energy projects expanded 59% annually, with incentives including the Solar Investment Tax Credit being funded. The country and SMEs that offer this operation are flourishing, with rooftop solar panels and household / commercial electrical systems.

Where one of these green solutions is in the interest of you, Natural Resources Canada's Solar Thermal and Solar Photovoltaic Energy Awareness Pages provide excellent information on this topic.

Everything must be washed from laundry to car. Yet consumers are much more prone to pollution and prefer to glow without the environmental pressure. One Green Business concept for them is to market environmentally friendly laundry items. It is another green business concept that can work well as a platform for e-commerce.

Going green is also a smart laundry service brand tactic. Commercial and residential cleaning SMEs still have "soft" market ideas with a continued increase in demand for cleaning services. You will only gain a competitive advantage by using environmentally friendly cleaning materials in your cleaning business.

Help them locally to locate something. Books like the 100-Mile-Diät have encouraged many people to think carefully where their food is grown and the harmful effects of buying goods which can be transported thousands of miles away.

People want local eco-friendly alternatives to their goods. To satisfy this need, farm markets have expanded in North America, from local beef, pork, or poultry to locally manufactured soap and cleaning materials. Speak to a local farmer group or butcher shop about local sales of your meat.

As energy costs rise and green becoming more mainstream, more people and SMEs want to green, but are unknown about the best course of action is required to be green. Green consultancy is also a business practice, and it is time to do so.

Green consultants have developed an action plan for their clients by examining the environment of their clients and analyzing their environmental strengths and weaknesses. For example, a home or business may use much more energy than is necessary for heating or cooling due to lack of weather-stripping, insulation, or incorrectly installed HVAC (Heating, Ventilation, and Air Conditioning) systems.

Some green consulting firms also offer event management services. The green business idea refers to the consulting firm that will ensure that every aspect of the event, from advertising to waste management, is handled in the most environmentally friendly manner.

Help them get in there. Scooters and Bikes Transportation is increasingly high pump prices reinforce another place of change for many people who need to go green. Scooters and bikes are a desirable "all-in-one" solution; as a scooter or bike rider, you can save money by becoming environmentally friendly, and if you get the kind of bike you need to pedal, you can also improve your health!

Therefore gas scooters and electric bikes continue to increase popularity, becoming a dealer might be the business idea you've been looking for. Statist estimates that sales of electric bicycles will reach 40 million units by 2023. There are several franchise opportunities available if you don't want to start a dealership from scratch.

Green Building Green Building is a trend packed with opportunities to start new green businesses. Construction small business-enterprise, architects, designers, and contractors may specialize in green construction. For example, the contractor may become a certified LEED professional; the designer may focus on the elements and materials that are least environmentally destructive.

And green building helps you work out for all kinds of green products that could be the foundation of small business, from water-saving to reclaimed wood.

Green Businesses Deliver More Than Profits Let's hopes you get excited about these green business ideas. You may not be costly, but you will have the pleasure of running a business that helps people lead greener lives and combines what you do with what you believe in.

3.2 Efficient Resource Management

For the past few years, the emissions issue has been hitting the headlines. Around the same time, countries are still struggling with certain forms of emissions, such as plastics and electronic waste (e-waste). The study finds that each nation produces 9.46 million tons of plastic waste annually, of which 40% remains uncollected. This also produces around two million tons (M.T.) of e-waste annually, according to the Global E-Waste Monitor 2017. Plastic and electronic waste has proven to be impossible to manage. Yet, any challenge has an advantage, and several business people have been able to capitalize on the need for recycling.

Increasing the consumer penetration of secondary raw materials is a core goal of the ambitious new European Commission plan to turn the E.U. economy into a more circular one. The kit would promote sustainability, increase resource usage, and open up new opportunities for secondary raw materials – goods that have been recovered from waste and are sold on the market for use in new items.

The re-injection of these products at the start of the product life cycle will reduce the cost of manufacturing and our environmental effects. Not only is this good for the world, but there's also a clear economic case for it. This will open up new business markets, facilitate innovative product creation, build opportunities, foster innovation, and boost economic growth.

The E.U. demand for recycled products and waste is underdeveloped. To order to understand the full value of all secondary raw materials, the Commission needs to help build up the case for further production, eliminate obstacles to their trade, strengthen waste management policies and increase trust in the quality of secondary raw materials through the creation of standards.

Overcoming barriers Confusion regarding the price of secondary raw materials may be a significant obstacle to their economic uptake. Standards are required to create confidence and to promote a common market for secondary raw materials in the E.U. The Commission will begin research to improve quality requirements for secondary raw materials where they are required, in particular plastics.

The Commission also wants to promote industrial symbiosis, where the waste or by-products of one industry are raw materials or resources for another. We have also suggested that the laws on by-products and end-of-waste status should be harmonized. The revised waste statutory framework would pave the groundwork for a simple legal position for by-products in all E.U. countries.

Waste transport between E.U. countries also entails substantial administrative burdens. They must take steps to promote the lawful shipping of waste while taking more action to counter illicit shipments.

Secondary raw materials as a primary investment field they find investments in secondary raw materials to be a priority. They are required in areas such as waste disposal systems, reverse logistics, storage or recycling, and emerging technology.

Via the Horizon 2020 development and innovation initiative, the E.U. has also sponsored initiatives on an EU-wide warehouse of secondary raw materials that aims to measure the supply and distribution of raw materials in society; the recycling of disposable electrical products; and the recycling of construction materials. 10 research projects based on the main goals of the European Research Agreement on Raw Materials will also be implemented by 2020.

Private funding has to be directed towards new prospects in the secondary raw materials industry. Re-use of building waste Building and demolition waste is one of the most massive amounts of pollution in Europe.

Improved recovery of essential raw materials (CRMs) is another resource that the circular economy program aims to explore. They are necessary since they are used in many critical manufacturing applications (such as medical equipment, propulsion systems), and ordinary mobile devices (such as smartphones), they cannot be replaced, so they also need to be manufactured from politically insecure countries.

Through the recovery of CRMs does not only open the door to new small business enterprises, but it will also help protect European access to CRMs.

Plastic recycling has still not met its full potential. Again, both smart design and careful processing will improve the rate of recycling of plastics and discourage landfilling, incineration, and the use of primary materials. The Commission will formulate a plan to tackle problems such as recyclability, biodegradability, and the existence of dangerous substances of concern in some plastics. This would increase the need for recycled plastics while increasing the demand for the services of plastic waste treatment firms.

Many chemicals have dangerous properties, and E.U. law now provides resources to control their risks. However, as more evidence is available as a result of technological advances, previously unclassified compounds may be recognized as dangerous or have their existing classification changed. The right balance must be reached between regulations requiring the recycling of products from waste that may contain harmful components for defined safe uses and the need to ensure that dangerous chemicals of concern are adequately handled. They will provide research and recommend solutions for the interaction between substances, goods, and waste regulations, including ways to enhance the monitoring of contents of concern in products.

The position of small and medium-sized enterprises. Although 45 percent of waste material from large businesses is being produced, this number falls to just 25 percent of small and medium-sized businesses (SMEs). The above face difficulties in taking the circular economy into account, since they cannot benefit from economies of scale such as big businesses.

As laid out in the 2014 Green Action Plan for Small and Medium-sized Businesses, we are working to help these firms, identify the obstacles they pose to better use of energy, and strengthen waste management.

In turn, SMEs, like social enterprises, would make a crucial contribution to the circular economy: they are primarily involved in fields such as recycling, restoration, and creativity.

3.3 Decrease the Carbon Footprint

Going green not only helps corporations protect the environment, but it also provides a range of financial and reputational incentives to help businesses expand.

Irrespective of whether you run a small or a big enterprise, there are ways you can become an eco-friendly brand. If you want to continue living up to your ethical commitments and save energy, learn how your enterprise can reduce the carbon footprint.

A big part of turning green is raising the carbon footprint. These tips will help you do precisely that, boosting productivity and making your enterprise more successful.

Running a profitable enterprise is challenging. Running a profitable enterprise that is responsible for pollution is much more complicated.

But just because our present free-market economic structure doesn't make it convenient to operate a profitable activity, it doesn't mean that the enterprise will end up in a global crisis. Climate change would devastate communities, devastate industries, and dramatically increase the cost of doing business as commodities grow scarcer and more costly.

Besides dwindling money, there are other concrete explanations for adopting measures that reduce the business 'greenhouse gas emissions. As one example, as the global threat escalates, foreign policymakers are expected to start enforcing more stringent environmental regulations –

implying that if you can neutralize your carbon emissions now, the business will be ahead of the curve. Also, research has shown that consumers favor eco-friendly products and have linked positive impacts on the world to employee happiness and morale.

Stay up-to-date with the latest energy efficiency tips. Lower the running costs and help protect the environment by staying up-to-date with the newest energy efficiency tips. Any action your enterprise takes to minimize its carbon footprint will grow with time and become a huge achievement that you will share with employees and consumers.

1. Shift to zero waste.

The real way we do industry – that is, by manufacturing, storing, processing, and disposing of goods – accounts for 42% of greenhouse gas emissions in the U.S. The introduction of a zero-waste strategy is a short-term, effective intervention that can effectively pay off the environment.

Moving towards zero waste starts with an evaluation of the current system, management, and disposal of the enterprise. During the audit, you can determine where the waste is being produced, how much, and where it is going. In there, you can set priorities for waste collection, avoidance and elimination, and enforce strategies to meet them.

Focus the energies on that, re-using and recycling – in that order – when implementing waste-reduction strategies.

Other forms of zero waste may include going paperless wherever possible, recycling obsolete appliances and office supplies, and using recycled, compostable, or recyclable wrapping materials. Refilling and recycling ink and toner cartridges will be a focus in the office's zero-waste policy. In essence, these containers are incredibly resource-intensive to make and can take thousands of years to decompose.

2. Harness clean sources of electricity.

Renewable fuels have been more popular in the past few years, primarily due to rising oil and gas costs and increasing fears regarding climate change. Given the limited existence of fossil fuels and the possibility that international climate change laws will be implemented shortly, businesses will now start monitoring and reducing their energy usage. It does not only offer economic gains but will give the industry a strategic advantage as climate regulations come into practice.

Although taking steps can entail an upfront investment, using renewable energy options such as solar power would save the business money in the long run.

When you are looking to buy or lease renewable energy equipment for on-site installation at your office, solar panels are the most apparent and potentially the most realistic choice. In addition to providing renewable, sustainable energy to your house, installing solar panels could qualify your enterprise for a federal tax credit.

When you do not own your property or have small rooms, you may start buying green electricity from your power supply. Many power providers offer the option to buy "carbon" energy on a limited premium basis in return for electricity generated from renewable sources. Based on the part of the world in which you are based, you will even be able to select your energy provider. In countries that require competition between electricity generators, you can opt to work with a supplier that specializes in the development of renewable energy sources.

3. Cut the pollution of corporate transport.

If it is air, automobile, or rail, industrial modes of transport are among the primary sources of greenhouse gas pollution. In the United States, the transport industry accounts for 29 percent of overall greenhouse gas emissions per year. By reducing infection and corporate travel costs, you will reduce the environmental effects of your enterprise while theoretically raising your bottom line.

If you don't think there is such a thing as business travel pollution, just ask the GHG Protocol, the body responsible for calculating this pollution. Large small business-enterprise such as IBM has implemented criteria from the organization to calculate their carbon footprint better. Travel carriers themselves are also working to reduce pollution.

Encourage the workers to ride on a bike by providing them with space to change and wash. Facilitate carpooling among colleagues with matching programs and incentives like preferred parking spots. Book more fuel-efficient seats on direct flights while boarding.

Of example, the easiest way to reduce corporate transport pollution is not to fly at all. Try encouraging workers to work from home to reduce pollution from commuting. If necessary, hold simulated meetings and training sessions instead of driving. It would also mean arranging for a speaker to come to the training site, rather than referring people to the training center.

Just Purchase Electric Enterprise Cars because your workers may need to move from A to B for jobs, you may want to provide them with safe, eco-friendly vehicles to help reduce their carbon footprint. If that is the case, you can only purchase electric vehicles over diesel cars. Not only do they run better, but they can also need less fuel, making both economic and environmental sense.

Encourage Alternative Ways of Transport Become a more responsible enterprise by allowing the workers to use different forms of travel while going to work. Of starters, provide workers with free parking, whether they use a carpool or consider using public transit or a bike to reduce their carbon footprint. Not only would it reduce pollution, but it may also shift the attitudes of the workers to climate change.

4. Prep and train workers.

Ultimately, the most crucial way to make the workplace more carbon-responsible is to involve the workers in the cause deliberately. Disheartened by grim predictions and jaded by relentless corporate green washing, it's easy for individuals to fall into climate panic, a feeling of powerlessness that prevents us from seriously resolving environmental problems.

To counter environmental discouragement and help inspire workers to recognize their potential to affect social change, teach the staff about carbon responsibility by making it unique. Once workers understand why they are told to change long-term habits, they are less likely to resist current eco-conscious initiatives.

To inspire the team leaders to take control of their carbon impact, promote insight into energy-saving strategies on the workplace at staff meetings, and set up feedback boxes. Try setting up a business funding program where you are practically replicating workplace contributions to eco-friendly non-profits. Enroll the staff in a sustainable subscription service such as Forest Founders, which allows users to use a digital dashboard to monitor and refute their carbon footprint by planting trees through a network of non-profit organizations such as the National Forest Foundation (NFF). Carbon monitoring subscription platforms will help to gasify the carbon responsibility cycle and experience firsthand the strength of their environmental effects.

Nature and capitalism should not have to be at odds with each other. By reducing the carbon footprint of your enterprise, you can reduce energy costs, boost employee morale, develop your brand's credibility as a pioneer in sustainability, and even increase your bottom line – all while maintaining the land and earth that we need to work on and prosper.

5. Allow your workers to work from home.

Of course, and if you want to reduce your electricity costs substantially, you will encourage your employees to work from home. It's convenient for workers to operate remotely due to cloud-based technologies. This addition to minimizing your power and water consumption, it will also help to reduce the carbon emissions of your workers, as they do not need to go to work every day.

Swap from Desktops to Laptops Do you know that laptops use an astounding 80 percent less power than desktop computers? That's a lot of energy if you employ a lot of workers. Become more energy efficient by exchanging desktops for laptops and saving a large amount of money per month.

Skype makes it possible for retailers to communicate with foreign consumers and will reduce their reliance on vehicles, aircraft, and trains. Plus, you can save your enterprise time and money as well.

6. Switch off Everything

You can ensure that your workers switch off their lamps and appliances at home every day to limit their consumption so that they can conveniently carry their energy-saving practices to work. Encourage any employee to power down and turn off his or her computer during the working day. You may also add motion-sensitive lighting so that it would only switch on when required and switch off due to inactivity.

3.4 Entrepreneurship Sustainability and Models

Climate change and environmental degradation pose the most significant challenge to humanity. Ecological problems, unmet social needs, and the financial crisis have increasingly affected the natural ecosystem and human society, creating a contradiction between economic development and environmental protection, negatively affecting sustainable development. The business community and the establishment have been considered to be the critical networks responsible for such problems, which call for new forms of business and social innovation.

Most countries have pursued economic development and, at the same time, have given priority to environmental protection. Business communities, entrepreneurs, and policymakers have shifted their interests to foster and develop new sustainable economic forms that can be labeled "green." However, due to the gradual acceptance by the public of the concept of sustainability, there has been a rapid increase in demand for green goods and services, thus demonstrating the ecological concern that is widely shared by the public. Entrepreneurs have been encouraged to pursue green entrepreneurship that generates economic and environmental benefits. Green entrepreneurship linking environmental, social, and financial objectives has been recognized as an effective method of building a sustainable society.

From the 1990s, green entrepreneurship has been a controversial field of research. Its concept could be identified in several related terms, such as eco-entrepreneurship, eco-entrepreneurship, environmental entrepreneurship, sustainable entrepreneurship, green entrepreneurship, ecological entrepreneurship, or sustainable entrepreneurship

Green entrepreneurship is used in the current study because it is a comprehensive concept that combines green entrepreneurship and sustainable development with the "triple bottom line" of the environment, society and the economy.

Compared to traditional entrepreneurship, green entrepreneurship has three unique characteristics:
- Environmental
- consumer green
- and policy support

Green Entrepreneurship is seen as a process that identifies, evaluates, and possesses entrepreneurial opportunities based on sustainable, environmentally friendly, and green principles. Green entrepreneurs are dedicated to innovating green products and technologies on the market to replace traditional products. It is indicated that green entrepreneurship must address usual economic problems and must, therefore, show concern about social responsibility and environmental issues and that individuals with significant ecological concerns and social responsibility are willing to engage green entrepreneurship. For most developing countries or areas, green entrepreneurship is collaborative. However, most green goods are relatively costly. Green entrepreneurship has a more extended investment period, greater social accountability, and thus depends more on political motivation and public support than traditional entrepreneurship. To tackle green entrepreneurs 'problems, strategic strategies include raising awareness of environmental issues in society, simplifying regulatory processes, hiring professional' new 'staff, and tracking non-green businesses with waste.

Green enterprise can be divided into two, respectively, existing SMEs, which have incorporated sustainable manufacturing practices or environmental management and new enterprises focused on natural and ecological resources, and which can, therefore, be classified as Green Enterprises. Both require highly green-trained and experienced professionals. However, developing and developed countries should also face the lack of highly green-trained and experienced professionals, which is a constraint on the green economy, and this situation has not improved significantly since 2011. The lack of professionals and the lack of university graduate in general, particularly those trained in science, technology, engineering, and mathematics (STEM) skills, challenged developed countries. However, the government in China has made great strides in moving economic growth to a "greener" viewpoint than previously, the absence of a consistent green capability structure and policy system has been a critical bottleneck in China's green transformation.

Work in the fields of social, political, and financial awareness has shown environmental deterioration in the sense of accelerated industrial and technical change due to increased economic growth. The scientific consensus on environmental improvements, especially from anthropogenic factors such as high greenhouse gas emissions, unhealthy consuming habits, and lifestyle, raise environmental issues within social and commercial networks. Several industries have incorporated research, often supported by institutions, to increase technological innovation, including new sustainable materials, green supply chains, circular economic models, low-carbon product processes, waste management digitization, passenger electrification, and light-duty vehicles, thereby addressing these concerns and helping to improve social conditions. These technological reforms at the business and industrial level in an uncertain environment or "change of natural environment" and the market opportunities (M.O.s) created by these environmental concerns, this paper aims to investigate the effects of these technological changes on an entrepreneur's intention to switch to green entrepreneurship. In particular, the objective of this paper is to identify behavioral patterns that can help map the purposes of changing to green entrepreneurship among recent business students, new entrepreneurial initiators, self-employed, and new start-up business owners. It also aims to understand the moderating effect of institutional forces (regulatory and normative beliefs) on factors that affect green entrepreneurial intentions among young people. The study proposes a psychological model that incorporates a push-pull-mooring (PPM) model to analyze the shifting intentions towards green entrepreneurship. The following section discusses a comprehensive literature review of green entrepreneurship in the context of the proposed theoretical framework.

Green Entrepreneurship and Push-Pull–Mooring (PPM)

The term "entrepreneur" refers to "taking the bridge initiative," which originated in France. Entrepreneurship refers to activities that transform creative ideas and resources into profitable opportunities for human enterprises to identify and exploit new products, processes, or markets. Also, entrepreneurship can produce different outcomes in a variety of ways, thereby promoting economic growth, increasing employment, and addressing environmental issues. Among the various forms, green entrepreneurship, which combines ecological, social, and financial objectives, has been considered to meet the demand for sustainable development significantly. Considerable interests in green entrepreneurship by scholars and the public have been evident since the 1990s, thus expanding its borders. In some ways, green entrepreneurship can be exchanged with eco-entrepreneurship, eco-entrepreneurship, environmental entrepreneurship, sustainable entrepreneurship, and green entrepreneurship.

Green entrepreneurship is referred to "the creation of new products for local customers, services or perspectives to meet environmental market opportunities," indicating that small business-enterprise is increasing competitive advantage through proactive environmental considerations. Green entrepreneurship is identified as a process that identifies, evaluates, and possesses entrepreneurial opportunities based on sustainable, environmentally friendly, and green principles. Moreover, green entrepreneurship means giving priority to the protection of the environment and the welfare of society when entrepreneurs turn conceptual products, technologies, and services into reality. It integrates business entrepreneurship and sustainable development, which must take into account the "triple bottom line" of the environment, society, and economy. Green entrepreneurship is argued to be understood as a form of social activity which seeks to protect the natural environment rather than merely to become a business. Green use has already been embraced by a growing public; thus, green entrepreneurs have growth opportunities. However, green business needs to tackle mainstream economic challenges and prioritizes corporate justice and environmental problems, meaning that SMEs with significant sustainability interests, social conscience, and green expertise are able to invest in green business.

In comparison with traditional entrepreneurs, green entrepreneurs must give priority to social responsibility and environmental issues during the development of conceptual products, technologies, and services.it is indicated that green entrepreneurs are committed to innovating green products and technologies on the market. Green entrepreneurship can, therefore, be defined as a kind of green behavior and a kind of switching routine that shifts the focus of entrepreneurs from economic profits to concerns about social responsibility and environmental issues, especially as traditional entrepreneurs to green entrepreneurs.

The PPM model has not been used to define green behavior as a useful conceptual framework for understanding the switching action of individuals. The PPM model originated from the "Laws of Migration" introduced in 1885 and was based on a push-pull model that was used to explain population migration. Within the PPM framework, the factors that induce the behavior of individuals to switch can be classified as a push, pull, and mooring factors. Push effects, as stressors, refer to harmful factors that force people away from their original location. In contrast, pull results see positive factors that lead prospective migrants to a particular destination.

Green consumption has increasingly been accepted by the public. As a result, green entrepreneurship has been widely prioritized on the economic policy agenda by many Western governments. Moreover, compared to traditional entrepreneurs, green entrepreneurs include environmental concerns, social responsibility, and green skills. Green entrepreneurs should face low scalability and extended return on investment periods that reduce interest on the part of financial providers. Additional costs have also been seen as a competitive disadvantage of green entrepreneurship. A common situation in which a shortage of highly green-trained and experienced professionals is constraining green entrepreneurship. However, the number of green start-ups has steadily increased worldwide, despite the need for green entrepreneurs to balance economic activities, social contexts, and environmental philosophy. The reasons why entrepreneurs intend to switch to green entrepreneurship should be investigated. Green entrepreneurship is a significant multidimensional construction that is determined by a diverse set of factors, including economic, social, and environmental objectives. The current study, therefore, identifies the factors that drive the switching behavior of entrepreneurs to green entrepreneurship, which is categorized as push, pull, and mooring factors.

CHAPTER 4: PRODUCTION CONVERSION

Conversion costs are a concept used in cost accounting that blends direct labor costs with fixed output costs. Conversion costs are other than the costs of raw components of a manufacturer's goods or production costs.

In other words, the processing or production costs to turn raw material into goods are the process costs.

The final conversion cost also occurs in the process cost estimate of a similar product.

The workers working on the small business assembly line are an example of forced labor.

Examples of overhead production include utility, secondary work, repairs and maintenance, deterioration, etc. in the production facilities of an organization.

In planning output, the first choice is which type of manufacturing process-the manner in which a good or service is produced-best fits the business objectives and customer demand. The type of product or service provided is an essential factor because multiple products that require specific manufacturing processes. There are usually three manufacturing types: mass manufacturing, mass adaptation, and customization.

The first decision in production planning includes which type of production process [the way an item or service is created] better suits the business's goals and customer demand. The type of products or service provided is an important consideration, as different goods that require different production processes. There are usually three forms of production: industrial production, mass innovation, and adaptation. Operational managers also define production processes in two ways concerning manufacturing:

(1) how inputs are transformed into products and

(2) How methods are synchronized.

Those forms of business providers also offer tailored services. For example, physicians will understand each patient's illnesses and conditions before designing a tailored treatment plan. Real estate agents may create a personalized service plan for each customer based on the type of house that they sell or want to buy.

Converting inputs into outputs as mentioned earlier, data (natural resources, raw materials, human resources, and capital) are translated into outputs (products or services). The inputs, the production cycle, and the final outputs are usually visible in the manufacturing sector.

Two simple processes are available to transform inputs into outputs. The essential data (natural resources, raw materials) in process manufacturing are separated into one or more processing outputs (products). For example, bauxite (input) is processed for aluminum extraction (production). The design process is the other way round. The essential components, such as natural resources, raw materials, or human capital, are either combined to manufacture or converted into products. For example, an aircraft is produced by integrating thousands of components that are its raw material inputs. Steelmakers use heat to save iron and other materials into stainless steel. Customers will play a part in the transition phase of services. For example, the tax planning service blends the tax preparer's expertise with the customer's financial details to complete the tax return.

Pacing A second aspect is walking when considering the manufacturing process. Long manufacturing cycles that can last days, weeks, or months without machinery shutdowns are continuously used. It is ideally suited for low-volume items with uniform components such as screws, glass, and paper. Some programs have an evolving mechanism, as well. An example is the local power provider. The costs per unit are small, so production is simple to schedule.

Machines are shut down and adjust at various times and manufacture many goods. This method is ideally suited to low-volume, high-variety products such as mass personalization or personalization goods. Workshops are examples of businesses that use a sporadic operation.

While some service SMEs use ongoing processes, most service SMEs rely on sporadic methods. For starters, a restaurant cooking gourmet meals, an operative physician, and an advertisement firm creates ad camps for business customers to tailor each customer's services. The periodic method is used. Notice that their 'development times' can be brief – either a grilled salmon or a physical inspection at a time.

1. Describe the various forms of manufacturing processes.
2. How do inputs become outputs in a variety of different products?

4.1 Market Fluctuations and Product Switching

Transition costs are the prices of modified goods, manufacturers, or products that a customer requires. While the most common switching cost is monetary, social, stress-based, and time-based switching costs do exist.

An increase in costs may take the form of significant time and energy received to move vendors, the possibility that regular activities of the business will be disrupted during the adjustment process, high cancelation fees, and the inability to procure equivalent substitutions for goods or services.

Key Takeaways

- The cost of change, as a result of modifying markers or products, is charged by customers.
- Firms with hard-to-master goods and limited competition can use the high cost of switching to increase profits.
- Individual firms that do not charge more top dollar switching costs guarantee long wait times and product delays and retains their customer base with a purely time-based switching expense.

How to move prices

Successful firms prefer to adopt tactics that require high-cost adjustment on the part of customers, to dissuade them from moving to the commodity, business, or service of a rival. For example, individual mobile telephone carriers charge extremely high cancelation fees for canceling contracts to reduce the risk of switching to another network. The latest proposals by various mobile phone providers to refund customers for cancelation fees have, however, annulled these switching prices.

Successful SMEs typically tend to use approaches that require high customer transition costs.

Price balancing is the building blocks of competitive competitiveness and business purchasing control. SMEs seek to ensure that switching costs are as high as possible for their clients, allowing them to trap consumers in their goods, and rise pricing each year without caring about competitive options with comparable attributes or identical pricing for their clients.

Shifting Costs can be divided into two categories: low and high costs. The price gap primarily depends on the quick transition and the equivalent competitive goods available.

Low Switching Cost

Businesses that have goods or services quickly reproduced by rivals at similar levels generally have small switching costs. The rising costs of clothing retailers are minimal; they can find clothing sales and compare prices quickly by walking from one shop to another. The rise of Internet retailers and fast distribution made it much easier for shoppers to purchase clothes on many online sites in their homes.

Substantial switching costs refer to businesses that produce specific goods with few alternatives that need significant effort to monitor their use. Consider Intuit Inc., which provides diverse tech applications for its clients. Since it takes a lot of time, energy, and instruction to know how to use Intuit apps, few customers are prepared to abandon Intuit.

High switching cost

Many Intuit apps are intertwined, providing consumers with extra functionalities and advantages, and very few businesses equal Intuit products 'size and usefulness. Small SMEs, who are the primary buyers of Intuit bookkeeping goods, can create confusion and threaten financial mistakes if they want to move from the software of Intuit. Such aspects generate high costs of switching and adhesiveness for Intuit goods, allowing the business to demand higher rates for its products.

4.2 Guarding Against Risk

When a business expands, multiple challenges and prospects need new approaches – what succeeded a year ago may not be the right strategy. Far too much, avoidable mistakes turn what a perfect business may have been into a ran.

To continue developing and succeed, it is essential to identify and resolve the common obstacles associated with development. Essentially, you ought to make sure that the actions you take now will not generate more challenges with the future itself. Good leadership lets you take advantage of the potential to build economic development for the future.

The guide addresses the particular risks and mistakes that impact emerging businesses more frequently and explains what you should do about them.

- Maintaining market share
- Looking ahead
- Money Flow and Financial Management
- Problem Solving
- Correct method
- Information
- Improvement

Keeping up on Competition

Market analysis is not a one-off as you launch the business. Business trends tend to shift, and market analysis will always be ongoing. Otherwise, you threaten decision-making based on out-of-date knowledge, which may lead to business loss.

The more active you become, the more rivals note and respond to what you do. Every day, an industry-leading bid could not be higher than usual a few months back.

Faithful consumers will find competing suppliers that offer a high price quickly.

In the era of products (and services), revenue growth and profit margins are shrinking. Knowing where the goods are in their lifecycles will allow you to improve productivity overall. You will need to invest in creativity to grow a variety of innovative, competitive products on the market.

Available knowledge may offer useful insights into industry dynamics and patterns. Your expertise will be much more critical as a growing business.

You should be able to create a detailed understanding of what consumers expect, how they behave, and which methods to the campaigns perform well.

It pays off to talk to the main clients. Your vendors and other industry partners may be critical customer intelligence sources. You will allow the workers to share their experience with clients and the sector. Active IT services may also promote the exchange and review of essential details, such as the purchasing habits of customers and priorities.

You may also want to perform further testing-for example, to test consumer responses to a new product. You could do it yourself, or you could hire an independent analyst or a market research firm.

Planning forward

Now is not necessarily right for you, the plan which made sense for you a year ago. The dynamics of the local market are continually changing due to which you need to review and revise your business strategy periodically.

When your business expands, your plan will adapt according to the changing circumstances. For instance, the emphasis will shift from winning new customers to creating productive relationships with current customers and optimizing growth. Existing commercial ties are also more efficient and can often produce stable cash flow. More unique relations can improve productivity, but profit margins can be smaller and not sustainable. See the Money Flow and Financial Planning tab in this section.

Around the same time, each organization must be alert to new opportunities. There are clear concerns that only current consumers can be counted on. The diversification of the client base increases these threats.

Not the only way to success is by adopting the same market pattern, but larger. Other structural alternatives, such as outsourcing or franchising, may provide better prospects for expansion.

This is important not to presume that your present popularity would mean that you will take advantage of these resources automatically. That significant change has to be prepared in the same way as a new start-up.

Make careful to be overly opportunistic – ask yourself how new plans match your talents and your overarching vision. Bear in mind that each new technology involves changing risks. This is worth reviewing the risks you face frequently and creating contingency plans.

Cash flow and financial management

Adequate cash flow controls are essential to any business. Cash shortages can be the most considerable force restricting growth, and overtrading can be dangerous for a growing business. Having the best possible use of the resources will be a central consideration in strategic preparation and assessments of potential prospects. You may continue to skip lucrative opportunities with minimal funding if seeking them means robbing the leading business of critical financing.

To optimize your free cash flow, each item of work capital should be carefully managed. Efficient credit management and strict debt protection are essential. You would also want to discuss increasing export debt funding.

Robust stock tracking and efficient supply management become increasingly critical as industries expand. Obsolete stock holdings can become an issue that needs to be periodically resolved. You may choose to partner with vendors to shorten distribution times or to move to just-in-time delivery supplies and systems.

Term planning lets you predict your financial requirements and have sufficient funding. Like several growing businesses, a crucial decision is to put in the funding needed to support further growth from outside investors.

Problem solving

Modern organizations often operate in constant crisis mode. Each day there are new issues that need to be addressed immediately, and management spends much of its time-solving problems.

This strategy just doesn't work as the business expands. While a short-term situation is still immediate, it does not matter about as much as you should. Spending your time to smooth an unhappy client may help to maintain this partnership-but instead of working on hiring the best salesperson can pave the groundwork of meaningful new sales for years to come.

For example, if you take precautions to ensure that your intellectual property is adequately secure; your business can be potentially at risk.

You may need to use more money to grow the brand if you concentrate on individual marketing strategies.

The definition of the primary growth factors is a helpful way to learn what to prioritize.

A structured management strategy focuses on managing managers, creating and building the management team

The marketing plan. The business policy. Instead of approaching each Problem as a specific problem, you build processes and frameworks that can improve handling in the future.

The right systems

All businesses generate and depend upon vast volumes of information – financial reports, client transactions, other business connections, employee documents, regulatory requirements, and so on. It is too difficult to manage – let alone effectively use – without the right tools.

Responsibilities and responsibilities can be assigned as the business expands, but you cannot operate efficiently without stable management information systems. Setting up the right infrastructure is a vital part of helping the business expands.

Also, documents, protocols, and processes are becoming increasingly necessary. The informality that can operate with one or two staff and a handful of customers in a growing business is not practicable. You need proper terms, specific requirements, efficient processes for jobs, etc.

Most growing SMEs considered one of the most successful ways to implement best practices using existing management practices. Quality management programs can play a significant part in driving progress and convincing larger consumers to focus on them.

Investing in the right structures is a short- and long-term project. You benefit from more effective processes every day. When you do want to sell the business, it will be an essential part of showing its worth that you have well managed, efficient programs.

Competences and attitudes

'Entrepreneurs have become the motivator behind modern SMEs. We are all too much the ones who hold them off.

The ability to help you start a business is not the same as the ability to make it grow. It is necessary not to dumb yourself too far into judging your skills. You can need the training to develop the skills and attitudes required by someone who leads to development.

To develop your business, you need to know how to delegate correctly, trust your management team, and keep every detail under control. Creativity and inspiration with undue intervention are all too natural to kill. As the business gets more dynamic, you must always improve your time management skills and learn to concentrate on what is essential.

When your business expands, you may need to support others. You may decide to assign particular areas of responsibility to separate experts or to name a non-executive director or two to strengthen the Council. As you choose to tackle a new possibility, someone who has expertise will be crucial.

Training to listen to advice-and take suggestions-is one of the toughest obstacles for many successful entrepreneurs. Yet it may also be necessary if you want to take advantage of your opportunities. Some businessmen often name someone else as **Managing Director or Chairman knowing their limits.**

Complacency increasing poses a significant challenge for a can business. Suppose you're always good merely because you were unwise in the past.

Review and update your business strategy periodically will allow you to consider and adapt to changing market conditions. See the on strategic plans in this section.

A current strategy lets you define the steps you need to improve your business and how it works, for example:

- Moving to vendors who will evolve along with you and meet your new goals. Consistent consistency and efficiency may be critical as the business expands, rather than just having the cheapest deal.

- Deal renegotiation to compensate for expanded quantity.
- Learning and workforce growth. Your position will also shift with the growth of the business. See the on skills and attitudes in this section.
- Make sure you keep emerging developments up-to-date.

You must devote yourself entirely to your plan even though it brings you out of your comfort zone. It may include challenging choices – for example, retirement to staff or the move of vendors for whom you have become mates. But unless you're able to do so, you risk offering a dangerous competitive drawback to your business.

4.3 The Art of Investing

It is not easy to run a business, particularly when capital is small. Unfortunately, you cannot run a corporation with your own abilities and determination. If you feel a little short in your market in the corporate world, it's time to start investing. Here are some suggestions that the average small business owner will continue to invest in the game.

1. Starting with Penny Stocks, Penny stock is a joint-stock sold on the market for less than a dollar. It's a highly volatile investment, but it's worth so little that it's a great place to start with new investors. Being a small business owner, you have an option to start trading a penny stock to learn the market and develop more skills by becoming an investor. Once you've got the hang of things, you may choose to continue experimenting with pennies or move on to different investments.
2. As an SME, there are many entities to consider with your business before making any kind of investment. To begin with this, you'll want to take a closer look at your business goals, business plan, debt burden, and financing.

Investing should be a way to increase income, not to supplement it.

In other words, taking the money you need for another part of your business to multiply your holdings is not smart. If the investment turns out to be at a loss, you've lost money on both your investment and your business, making it hard to recover, especially if the cash flow is low. Instead, keep in mind the best interests of your business when investing. Use surplus profits to make investment payments, and always remember that investing should not be treated as gambling.

3. Diversify Portfolios you still have a chance to make profit from each other if one of your stocks is devalued. This reduces the net financial risk and allows you to protect the business interests.

4. Consider Mutual Funds There is a level of risk and return that must be taken into account when making sound investments and always a balance must be created. The lower the chance, the better – makes investments in a mutual fund a perfect place to start.

Hundreds of inventories have been collected in one place and the fund manager puts money into the fund to boost the growth rate. The probability that such an investment will lose money is small, which makes it an invaluable incentive. With your stocks growing slowly, you can consider the ups and downs of the market and plan for more important projects.

5. Keeping time on your side is by no means a fast, rich scheme although it is regarded like that by many amateur investors. It's a long-term game where people who are waiting get the best returns. Furthermore, it is not always an indication when things look bad on the market that you are expected to withdraw your money. After the bear

market, the resulting yields are often much higher, but only for those who wait the right time to sell. Trying to pull out your savings when the economy is incorrect and position them in the best way makes you miss some of the best returns.

6. Leverage can actually increase the income, but it is important to remember that it can also go the other direction. It increases your expenses as much as your gains, and when you are in the market, that will be a little too much to enjoy. If things go wrong, the broker may request a margin call demanding that the lender raise additional cash to pay for the shortfall.

7. Reduce taxation and costs. Trading and trading in a business setting are sadly not safe. Many undisclosed costs and taxes have to be taken into account. Such payments can equate to up to 30 percent of your profits if you don't manage it from the outset, so know how the expenses can be reduced. Until investing, look at the fees and taxes involved and see if the rates reflect the risk.

This should not have to be taken lightly. When you go to the market for your small business, you put a lot of money on the table and a sequence of wrong decisions will get you so far that it'll be difficult to recover. Carefully enter the market and cover all the bases to make sure you win.

4.4 Availability of Tax Breaks and Financing

Business owners have a few days to register in the tax season on their calendars: March 15 to file corporate returns, and March 17 to have a drink at the local Irish pub. Sadly, we can only give recommendations on the former, but we have good news for business owners that "are small business credits tax deductible? "If you borrowed money last year, you will subtract some of your low business debt payments.

Basics

The debt contributions shall be split into an amount of interest and amount of the balance of the loan. The part of the investment which goes into importance is tax-exempt, but the portion which is paid out of cash is not excluded from the loan.

But let's assume, for example, that you spend $1,000 a month for a business loan. $300 goes to debt and $700 to the balance of the loan. You will subtract $300 a month for interest, but no tax deduction is necessary for the remainder.

It reduces the amount of money you pay taxes by making the deduction. That is not the same as raising the charges by the deduction number. For example, if you spend $3,600 a year in interest ($300 to 12) and expected to record $100,000 in tax revenue, the amount would drop to $96,400 after the deduction. When you pay a premium of 21%, the bill would be $20,244 (with interest deducted) equivalent to $21,000 (with no interest deducted), and the difference would be $756. You won't save as much as your discount, but making tax-deductible on small business loans remains a significant economic boost.

The Fine Print

However, the interest contribution becomes tax-free even after you satisfy the following criteria.

- You have to be fully liable for the loans to get a bond signed.
- Plan to pay back the capital.
- Have an actual debtor and lender partnership. When you borrow from a partner or family member, use a signed promissory note that displays the interest rate and a simple repayment plan. When not, your deduction can be rejected by the IRS.

- Spend something on loan for your business. You cannot take the tax deduction because you leave the money in the bank.

Do corporate interest premiums have a tax deduction on all forms of loans? The good news is yes; virtually some form of business loan requiring interest makes a deduction. Remember if such deductions can be extended to specific credit scenarios to ensure you gain full tax support:

- Period – lengthy revolving loans are generally arranged to make you pay further interest from an early point, which provides that the deductible would at first be higher but would grow reduced with time. The downside is that as soon as you pay taxes, you get an annual discount.
- Credit Lines – If a lender offers you a lending line on request, you simply pay interest (and earn a deduction) from the funds that you raise each year. Accessible sources of financing could work to your competitive benefit depending on your market needs and tax burden.
- Short-term loans – When a loan is expected to be taken off over a year, you will subtract the undivided interest from your income, which is typical with other small business loans. Smart business owners will use this broad tax allowance to fund their performance, just like a line of credit.
- Personal loans – As long as private loans are duly reported, interest is entirely deductible to us (as outlined above). When split between corporate and personal use, the deduction must be divided accordingly.
- Extension Loans – Loans for the acquisition of another business are also used. The loan interest is payable if you intend to operate the service. If you do not wish to do so, your contribution is considered an "investment," and your

interest will not be tax-deductible. In this situation, a tax expert is better approached.

The Exceptions

'Will tax deductions be deductible? "It's confusing because of debt agreements where the corporate income cannot subtract interest. Until you enter into any debt deal, you will learn about these exceptions: is small business loans tax deductible? Yeah, in most situations. In having this tax deduction, your interest costs will be a bit more manageable, and the initial tax returns a little less, yeah, taxable.

Tax time takes away from our highest. A minor saving grace is a general concept that you can demand deductions at any rate when earning revenue. Some of these deductions – payroll, equipment, salaries, and services – are straightforward, but there are five that you may not be sure of.

Refinanced allowances – The principal will no longer be forgiven if you receive a second loan from the same lender and use it for paying the debt on the initial loan. Nevertheless, the interest you paid on the second loan will also be deducted.

Commercial Real Estate – When you buy commercial properties with borrowing, you will not subtract the origination costs and the specific points as business expenditures. Instead, you will add this to the overall cost of the house. You will deduct them as part of the asset loss over time.

Standby Payments – The IRS does not consider this fee as a form of interest tax, and it cannot be withheld because the lender pays you a premium to keep the funds in standby.

Capitalized interest – If you rely on borrowing to fund the construction of a long-term asset, potentially a home, you have to apply the capitalized interest to the expense of the house instead of deducting it from the tax bill.

Any debt on the borrowings, including liability on business loans, overdrafts, and other lending services, will be excluded. This may sound trivial, but you can eliminate additional interest costs that may be easily ignored.

Secondly, any debt accrued on a business loan but not paid by June 30 will be deducted.

Third, often small business owners use personal loans or their credit cards to finance their businesses. And because the business itself does not pay interest payments but the corporate owner, you can claim a refund for the interest in your income tax.

Small businesses do not fail to demand depreciation – the valuation reduction and wear and tear on the business's properties are removed.

Assets typically tend to be phased down slowly for many years, but SMEs are entitled to an instant tax write-off on any asset up to $6500 worth of assets. For instance, if the business bought a $4000 machine in the current tax year, the business might demand an automatic 100% exemption from tax while you are filing the return.

Small SMEs also have substantial depreciation discounts as they purchase new cars.

SMEs will depreciate cars, trucks, and vans quicker than others. We take a 100% refund on the first $5,000 in car purchases and will then depreciate the balance by 15% in the year we acquired it. Therefore a $14,000 vehicle will receive a $6350 tax-deductible in the buying year. (If the car costs less than $6500, the overall deduction under instantaneously defined write-off rules of the instantaneous asset will be claimed.) However, the government wants to remove those discounts, in compliance with the general depreciation law. The initial deductible on a $14,000 car will instead fall to $4200.

However, as per the law of general deflation, the government wants to withdraw these concessions and bring them back on January 1. If that occurs, the initial $14,000 vehicle deduction will be reduced to $4,200.

Tax season is a perfect chance to stock up and sees if you are available for any trade deduction – whatever you make, import, buy and purchase or sell for your business.

For a tax deduction, you will write off any lost, destroyed, or expired stock. When your portfolio price increases by more than $5000, you need to weigh your trading stock's increase of value into account while figuring out your taxable profits for the year. When the valuation of the stock at the end of the year is higher than at the outset, the increase will be reflected in the taxable profits. Nevertheless, if the stock is worthless, you are entitled to a discount.

The stock's price, its present sale value, and its future value are three different forms of valuation. You will pick which piece of stock to use, helping to optimize deductions.

It's still bad news for a small enterprise when debtors don't pay for the goods or services they have sold. At least there is a slight silver lining – a tax refund on the reduced debt may be sought.

A reduced debt is a mortgage you have been in mortgage for 12 months or more and makes a strong effort to repay. It pays to add to the unpaid factures and locate poor debts and to write them off on June 30 before the tax year.

CHAPTER 5: PSYCHOLOGY OF ENTREPRENEUR

Much work has been conducted on the psychological traits typically exhibited by an entrepreneur. There is no such thing as an "entrepreneurial temperament," and the internal makeup of capable businessmen is very different. Nonetheless, there are some reasonably straightforward features that which have been mentioned below that are representative of other businesses. It is the basis for attributes like an ability to be their manager and also for qualities such as a willingness to seek suggestions from other people who may be useful.

Firstly, what does the term 'entrepreneur' mean as distinct from being 'self-employed' and running your own business? Within this debate, a contractor is always motivated by ingenuity, development in his individual SME, and income. In this case, self-employment is typically based on the owner fulfilling his ambitions and the primary source of revenue for his job.

And what are some of the entrepreneur's characteristics?

Firstly, they need to be effective. It applies to the desire for success to achieve a feeling of personal accomplishment. Entrepreneurs prefer to pick and work hard on SME ventures with small chances of success or a significant opportunity for individual achievement and happiness, but without the possibility of unnecessary loss. Entrepreneurs in my experience are looking for opportunities, but typically don't get interested in SMEs where growth and profitability are minimal. There is no hope that they can develop a sense of personal success.

This is also frustrating for business people to consider that other individuals in their SMEs do not seek the same accomplishment. This is critically critical in a productive entrepreneurial enterprise that critical stakeholders agree on values, mission, and business goals. However, workers may still make an affirmative commitment to the business without feeling the same desire for recognition and personal results.

The second general attribute is what is known as an internal control locus. The locus of influence refers to the understanding of a person of the triggers of events in their lives. An internal locus of authority means you assume that the world is controlled by your actions; in this case, the success of your organization. This is, chance and circumstance do not determine what happens, and success or loss comes from the skill and experience of an entrepreneur. This will increase the confidence of an entrepreneur in making business decisions. Often it will lead to a loss, though, if projects take longer or cost more than they had wished for even though there are valid explanations.

The third general attribute is an inconsistency and confusion response. This refers to the ability and security of a person to determine with insufficient or uncertain knowledge. Unfinished demand, cash flow, competition, and IP growth knowledge is often characteristic of a business enterprise. Nevertheless, choices are made, and business people typically find them comfortable. Enterprises can find an uncertain business situation prudent, even fun, and if things tick, it may seem dull. However, a phase of restructuring at certain stages of business growth may be of value to the SME, if not particularly challenging to an entrepreneur.

A fourth common trait is what is considered a tendency to take the risk. This means that the entrepreneur is actively seeking risky ventures or activities and is more likely to take risks. An important aspect here, though, is measured uncertainties, not impulsive actions. There is a distinction between a problematic but measured decision and a gamble. SMEs face a chance of being propensity, but they indeed don't find themselves to be very dangerous, even though some do. We seem to see it differently than most.

To end, this is a concise summary of some of an entrepreneur's psychological attributes, not completely necessary or necessarily shown.

5.1 Leadership Skills of the Entrepreneur

Although every entrepreneur is exceptional and able to achieve success on its own, they all need to develop those essential characteristics daily. Leadership is difficult to describe, and effective leadership even more challenging. But you are a great leader if you can get people to follow you through the ends of the earth. This is the best leadership ability any business owner wants to learn in his work and home lives.

The ability to handle scrutiny will be one of the greatest assets. And if you do it correctly, this criticism can be turned into action. If people don't like an idea, an entrepreneur with excellent leadership skills will use negative feedback to find ways to improve. Leaders like thick skin; thank you for paving the way for success.

Here are some useful tips for handling criticism:

1. be polite still.

The offended and defensive act is only unprofessional. This does nothing but give you and your business an evil eye. People are going to presume that you are not cut out for your role.

2. You don't always think you're right.

All make mistakes (including the best SMEs). Don't be so stubborn, mainly if they don't show you the answers you want to see. Taking note of the ideas of others, even though you disagree with them.

3. Record the helpful input.

All you can do for an anonymous internet user "you suck" message. Only the guidance that is well thought out or that comes from someone who wishes you to excel. All of the most legendary executives of our day share one thing in common: Love. "Let the vibration of others 'views block out your inner vision." Being an enterprise is not a fainthearted thing to do because if you think about it, there is a significant gap between business owners who are out for money and people who enjoy what they are doing. The latter is motivated by the sense of achievement and what it takes to create something bigger than itself.

There are many wrong reasons for starting a business. Yet there is only one actual, genuine cause, and I think you know what that is: it's to change the world. If you are very concerned about your job, this shows. Your faith and passion are infectious, and many cannot help but want to be part of it. Whether you recruit new workers to help you along or making a sales pitch for a prospective buyer or investor, your passion is the measure of your success.

Don't you find your client passionate? That's all right! Working in a market that you enjoy is excellent if only so you can devote a lot of time working on it. But if you're not 100% sure about what you're doing, you may want to be a businessman or your boss. The argument is that it is more than money to create your enterprise. When your obsession is just for the big bucks, your customers will sense it, and you will still want more and never get to it.

Capacity to work with like-minded individuals Strong communication abilities helps to engage with others. It's all about coordination, after all. Keep yourself in contact with other enterprise owners—many real-life experiences from people who try to make a difference through help. You can find a mentor or other related entrepreneurs with whom you can share your ideas and frustrations.

Ninety percent of leadership is the opportunity to express something that people want. Like-minded people achieve the same outcomes.

Consider entering a peer review to get fresh ideas from other founders and to get advice from individuals of diverse viewpoints. These ties can prove useful in the future and enable you to improve leadership skills. You should have the resources you need to achieve your targets when you manage the business environment.

If you join a peer advisory community, it is essential to learn if the representative has personally been in the shoes of the owner. You don't want to be in a party where the chief has no training or organizational skills. The right peer leadership groups encourage you to gain input from other Entrepreneurs and develop morale, exchange insights, and have suggestions with each other.

How are these classes found?

Submissions and Testimonials: Continue here, and you quickly see how the members of such categories have achieved positive benefits for their clients. You can speak to existing members, but you can still seek to locate past members. Tell them blankly, "Why have you been leaving? "The solution will allow you to match better.

Books and Speakers: If you know that they have achieved performance, get insight into the attitude, methodology, and temperament of a community member. Books will give you a look into your past and how the obstacles have been resolved. Seminars and conferences can contribute to an introduction. Furthermore, most speakers are prepared to give a sort of tutorial for such activities. Only be careful. A brilliant speaker or writer isn't necessarily a perfect leader at a party.

When you are not ready for a peer support group, try looking for a mentor. A business coach/mentor gives a client community some of the same advantages, but at a much more personal stage.

A coach should provide options when:

- Work and life are difficult to navigate.
- You want to recruit a new squad or have issues with your existing staff.
- You're more depressed and exhausted than committed and excited about your work.
- You have trouble knowing your business plans.
- You are untrustworthy.

5.2 The Sense of Responsibility and Crisis Management

A market crisis could strike any enterprise at any moment. You also learn today that the number of insolvencies is growing. What causes have also contributed to liquidation, it does even kill the places of work and the ideals established by the businesses.

In addition to the degradation of ideals and places of employment, it is often worth remembering the human tragedies of new owners and workers.

That is why an enterprise owner should understand and be able to handle a business situation as early as possible.

And the size of an organization does not make a disaster inevitable. No, we saw only big corporations heading down the tube.

Enterprise Catastrophe Reasons

The origins of market problems differ very much as SMEs do. The factors of the market crisis may, however, be divided into separate fields.

- Markets and the economic downturn
- Lack of viable goods
- Management errors
- Restructuring challenges
- Lack of strategic and organizational business strategy
- Lack of performance monitoring or continuing review
- Lack of expenses/cost accounting
- The average employee in poor terms
- Customer communication insufficient and feedback procedure
- Lack of sourcing of items
- In most cases of a business failure, it can be concluded that there were not only one of these triggers, but a combination of any or both of them.

For a startup enterprise, the above list also has reasons that entrepreneurs must be mindful of.

Crisis symptoms (crises/alarm signals)

Dependency on only one or two customers, false plan, Optimism, and dedication as a supplement to managing. Advertising is used on a casual basis.

Loan criteria for startups are being underestimated for the launch process, and new bus 'creators are being overlooked. Hardships are almost automatic. As a checklist of warning signs, the following list can be included.

Market Information on the growth and scale of the business comes primarily from unintended customer meetings and sales department meetings.

Broad market dynamics are only understood incompletely, and you only know your rivals poorly. You are not aware of the growth of the industries of your most valuable customers.

No policy. Measurable estimates are not specified for forecasting. No operating strengths and disadvantages are identified. It is only conceivable to determine which goods and consumer segments attain the level of revenue and productivity with tremendous effort. There are no daily meetings with main stakeholders about their contentment, needs, and future innovations. Contrary to your rivals, you do not make a convincing point on your business 'advantages.

Market growth stagnates or declines your market fewer to existing consumers, so you risk it. You may not know how much consumers you produce whose selling amount

You may not realize or are unwilling to assess dependency on large customers; big and small customers are analyzed with the same strength irrespective of productivity.

Sales are costly as they are challenging to assemble. The rate of progress is through you should only mention with very high commitment the ten most valuable customers with sales volume and a wide margin.

Gross prices are more significant than sales. Cost increases are higher than the average price rises. Cost changes cannot be known in depth. The estimated value is used for price estimation. Complete expense estimates are carried out. There is no daily test and, if possible, no change in the determined rates.

Accountancy is not used as a monitoring and intelligence tool. You do not know precisely lower price thresholds economic analyses often take place incorrectly and are not evaluated, or the tests fail to return the condition correctly.

The contribution caps are not established. Income growth is unfavorable you do not know which sub-areas are receiving profit or loss Liquidity your cash is back with stagnating/declining profits accounts receivable rise faster than revenues overdue account receivables rise within overall accounts receivable

Overdue accounts receivable decreases

There is no organizational map available. Workflows are not recorded, and some work is carried out indefinitely and indefinitely.

The administration takes all decisions — the board. Items and scopes of the enterprise are little known to staff and clients.

High workplace variability and high disease levels (> 10%) are common. The incentive for workers to sink is obvious.

With an ERP-System, workers will still look at the stored records in case of doubt.

Employees collect market strategy knowledge from magazines and media, but not from enterprise executives.

Furthermore, business managers must have the experience as an enterprise expert (in particular: finance and accounting) or must ensure that this expertise is accessible to businesses.

Every entrepreneur should know his revenue and cost structure and appreciate his tax advisor and controller's evaluations. Otherwise, the contractor can't decide how it goes above the average.

Additional indicators of an already existing or imminent recession are:

- business equity would have absorbed profits over the short-term
- the obligation is not related to income capacity (interest and repayment will no longer be made)
- Payables will now be met with tremendous difficulties (attention: bankruptcy is the cause in many jurisdictions!)

- Accountancy gaps (to rapidly rising businesses are now at risk. Thus in the phases of high development, the organizational structure and the required resources must expand.

It is the main issue itself, as capacity preparation and capability expansion is a concern dependent on constantly shifting estimates.

Overcapacity is built up rapidly and can only be seen as demand is abruptly smaller.

Consolidation steps are also to be used to evaluate potential false findings and to implement effective countermeasures. Then you must analyze the past, and only then can you prepare the future.

Disaster measures

Select anyone to assist you with your accounting and management, who can configure the controls and supply you with some useful knowledge.

Talk to your bank and prominent vendors early and explain your condition, the sooner, the better. In most situations, transparency to those involved will solve the problem.

Using all the alternatives to get money, just don't sell yourself. You must monitor the accounts receivables and obtain receivables more efficiently.

Factoring is a way if you need money desperately. When you have a bank account overdraft status, you ask me to refinance it into a long-term loan, which would reduce your interest spending.

You can be able to capitalize on government grants to continue operating for your business.

Nonetheless, you do not rely on government funding. The business may not be worthy. Strengthen the operating structure (customer service, order processing).

Beware of the enterprise's solvency, and it's most critical first. The willingness to perform is essential to the second stage.

If you have established these conditions for your business 'sustainability, you can proceed to the third stage, the expansion or the raise of the gross profit.

These three are going to be flipped back and forth in real life.

Crisis management actions-Using an enterprise ratio method, which tells you the most relevant market figures. The most important ratios are:

- Capital ratio
- Return on Revenue
- Cash Flow Margin

In turn, you can have your eyes set on the following:

- cash on hand (must be at least on short-term payable height)-short- and medium-term payables
- Gross payments receivables (money you lend to your client on long contract periods, you can't work, meaning: the sooner you get, the best for you) Keep the system small and precise.

Each of them is the incoming instructions. Don't blast the power prematurely. Pay attention to details that let you handle your business.

You primarily learn these details from your everyday job; you just need to make it useful.

And if your corporation is running well, you should keep everything in your organization under control so it will change quickly.

Tolerate no mistakes such as 'no time,' 'it's working pretty good right now,' "I've got it in my brain," 'My men are going to do everything.'

You are the boss (or at least anyone of significant influence) and the one who primarily determines the business's destiny. Start with proper evidence. Go forward with a positive experience.

For example, in these cases, nobody has a crystal ball to recognize a problem on the horizon. However, you should be cautious in the creation and execution of programs that no signs of impending issues. Entrepreneurs need collaborative networking devices, foresight, and innovative thinking by their hands.

You don't even need the crystal ball when it comes to it. Just talk about what could go wrong and what it would feel like. So at least develop a simple crisis management strategy with the guidance of key personnel that can be executed as necessary.

Social networking has undoubtedly revolutionized business-to-customer interactions. This is true of customer service. However, you can and can still use these platforms to define and handle future enterprise crises.

Using social media networks for the enterprise to cool turbulent waters, not supporters of the opposition. It is quick to take a defensive stance and protect the credibility of the enterprise when it is threatened. The safest way, though, is to "Hot" stay:

- Listen: hear what people think. Track exchanges and enterprise comparisons.
- Participation: remain involved in conversation even though you say, "We're listening, and thank you for your feedback."

- Transparency: no matter what you're doing, certainly don't erase reviews on your Facebook account, blog, or anything else only because they are essential. The opponent can just backfire if he attempts to censor.

At least always start by addressing the issue. Radio silence normally inflames passions that are still agitated. This produces more drama. It is reasonable that you do not comment until you have collected more accurate details. Nonetheless, just a comment "we are mindful of the problem and conduct our internal analysis, and we will address more when we finish the process" helps convince the viewers that you are at the top of the matter.

Hearing the enterprise profoundly can be very unpleasant and may induce severe anxiety. One likes to hear someone else condemn them negatively, mainly though you know the allegations are real.

However, that's the best step to take. Managing a national outcry is like a delicate negotiation, except with an anonymous, faceless audience. And like any professional negotiator, the first requirement is to listen attentively to the other argument.

Often all it takes is your full attention and apologies to turn an unhappy customer into an appreciated user. The angry customer needs to be heard many times. All wins if you can stop the stampede before it happens. When you can't, you've at least learned enough to know the stakes.

If there are a flaring temper and critique, you might want to take advice from your advisory board. Try creating your ad hoc "elderly" committee. Look for others who work or have more expertise in your profession than you are (ideally, both). These people will tell you all about the next best move.

Based on advisors 'comments, you might get contrary advice. You will have to deal with these disputes eventually. You are taking into account the duration and understanding of these inconsistent claims and using your instincts to determine whether to proceed.

If fire travels much quicker than you can put it out in such fever-pitch fights, hire a skilled public relations agency. If civil or criminal law is a possible result, retain the services of a corporate law firm with expertise within your jurisdiction. Do not make things harder by attempting to control a still out of balance situation.

In the end, all you can do, because everyone else can trust you to do are make the right decision. Then you can claim responsibility for the implications of this action. Take the opportunity to listen to the opponents and search for the correct advice you can before taking the final call.

You now have an outline of potential enterprise distress symptoms. Do not take this essay too literally and its implications. But don't pretend that the threat isn't there, either.

Only because the sales level has dropped a little within a month does not mean that you are on the road to a crisis. Deviations in the numbers will also allow you to examine more deeply.

You must be prepared for a disaster as an enterprise owner. You will encounter a range of losses, ranging from moderate uncertainty and disappointment to category five, which are undermining the very existence of the enterprise.

The management in a crisis requires attentiveness, careful preparation, and well-developed organizational processes.

5.3 Effective Employee Management

Any small business treats HR well like it can handle fire safety: the everyday burden of the enterprise can cause them to neglect even the simple measures to keep them compliant, and when an issue sparks, it is forced to scramble.

To order to save money, data reveals that 54% of small businesses work with workers themselves. Yet Entrepreneurs also recognize that they will be better off investing money on revenue, infrastructure, and other roles.

Therefore, many of the workers who conduct HR activities are not trained. According to ADP's Ad Hoc Human Resource Management Report, 70% of SMEs with 5 to 49 workers apply HR to workers 'workload with little to no expertise with workplace problems. Such ad-hoc HR administrators undertake positions, including office managers and chief executive officers, about 23% of the time, while 12% work in accounting.

While they spend 20% of their time on workplace issues, 81% of them do not focus on HR expertise, while 82% do not have structured HR training, ADP. Just 20 percent have faith in their ability to handle HR without fault. Surprisingly, less than 50 percent of small-business owners are very sure about how their SMEs handle HR in a payroll service study by Paychex. Business audiences say that businesses with less than 20 employees are much best off when the employer transfers HR duties to others within the firm. Yet it's not only necessary for business leaders to start delegating in good time, but also to think who they can trust and how they can support those people to succeed.

The first question is when to delegate

Of course, when will the owner continue to empower? Businesses need some sort of HR feature until they recruit their first employees. However, over and above simple considerations such as exact compensation and enforcement, small SMEs rely on their shareholders for sustainability in ways that go far beyond administration.

Small-business HR professionals, managers, and advisors agree: often, the time to start delegating is about the employee. We do not, however, base this calculation on any type. Instead, they say it is at this time that members of an organization learn that their resources can be spent on other issues more advantageously.

There are other, more visible indicators that owners need HR assistance. If you recruit four managers individually, you need a similar strategy. Standardization increases productivity in different ways, such as recruiting and control of benefits. Owners have also been on the lookout for inefficiencies, and one of his most important contributions was to establish a textbook detailing many enterprise practices early on.

The overall pace of enterprise and sales always leads to the determination as to how an employer should assign HR.

But with the aid of a consultant, the management of the HR department of the group soon became a plum, despite the high turnover rate of the sector. You are moving from 55 workers to 70, and then you have so much training and onboarding.

The original approach was to include a specialist to ensure conformity and support recruitment. Since the organization spent too much in training its workers to work correctly. She employed a full-time HR generalist less than one year after Synergy opened its third facility in 2015. We had to move these candidates quicker, with more than 70 workers in a high-turnover environment. We needed to get them reviewed and washed [by the Justice Department] quickly; we needed to get them to places to prepare more efficiently.

Choose the Correct individual

Many enterprise owners err based on their position instead of their expertise as they want to assign HR.

Sadly, they pick individuals who are not more eligible than any other office manager. They need to find someone who can keep it private, be coordinated administratively, and be an empathic listener and guide for workers.

It seems to me that the HR director wants to be the production manager, particularly for a small organization, and they need to have some expertise and chops. You're looking for someone who understands, [and] works in and appreciates the small business.

For a small business HR guy, it is critically important to have excellent human skills. They're most much the ones that bring bad news.

The best choice requires the selection of the individual with the best ability – and then the preparation of that child. HR needs tremendous experience, and an enterprise owner may make one of the worst decisions in outsourcing HR duties to someone who has no practical training at least.

Small businesses have other options to use for support. Most countries provide courses and technological assistance.

When he took over the duties of Likeable HR (initially working for a different role), the owners of the business left the way to introduce him to other SMEs, who were doing the kind of work he began to do.

Allowing him time to study and improve made a massive difference in his career. Owners will help their HR employees to find someone passionate about it.

In addition to dispute management, cognitive maturity, and a diversity of viewpoints on topics, such as the view of the enterprise and the view of the individual, is both essential HR skills.

If someone has a lousy job, you have to know if the input has been provided. Those cognitive patterns do not necessarily apply to everyone, he claims, and enterprise leaders will note that you cannot go to school for any Hours.

Education will not be limited to anyone approved for the HR service. In smaller businesses, for instance, the most important people are hiring. This means that they do need training. Administration duties may be assigned, but other items remain with the managers.

Enterprise proprietors are not fired until a point individual is appointed for HR. As noted, the needs of a shift as it expand and create more and more dynamic areas and jobs. You will re-evaluate each year or so. It is probably time for you to push [HR responsibility] beyond your office manager if you have reached 20 people, three of them remotely.

It claims that businesses with 25 or more staff will have someone with HR experience at least. When not, they would consider the cost-effectiveness of outsourcing. You need a full-time HR guy who can handle anything, even handling some outsourcing, once you get to 75 or 100 employees.

There are opportunities open to enterprise owners, despite their initial steps in HR, Speak to those in the field. Check for local HR parties. Speak to a trustworthy lawyer. And, she said, make sure your HR employee is part of your strategic thinking. An HR worker who just does the job is the wrong guy.

5.4 Playing a Fatherly Role

Without a doubt, a competitive spirit can be both a blessing and a curse. Too aggressive can destroy relationships and lead to personal and professional failure. Nevertheless, ignoring rivalry will deter you from thriving in life. While you can stop being overly competitive when working with someone else, a competitive spirit is essential with business success. There are three reasons why you need a competitive entrepreneurial spirit.

Competitors see challenges as incentives to improve an organization. Beginning a long, complicated cycle with many barriers and hurdles to resolve is a challenge. However, good athletes realize that such obstacles and difficulties will only improve them.

Much as a weight life is only improved by gradually raising the weight it seeks to lift, businessmen are improved by facing ever more obstacles. Even if the challenges growing to appear overwhelming at times, real entrepreneurs see them as opportunities for success; ambitious businesses also have a success philosophy that lets them never stop and pursue prospects for innovation, advancement, and change.

Competitors will not abandon Good competitors see life as a long race. Although this can also have adverse consequences as it spills into personal partnerships, successful people in business prefer to break apart and take losses when they do not give up. Although a professional competitor aims to win any game or event, he also knows that all victories and injuries are associated with even a winning season. But the biggest winners have a decent share of lost seasons. That is not a mentality where they want to lose or just take it; it means a single defeat or disappointment or even a season of suffering.

Competitive people in business see it commonly. Instead of being frustrated by disappointment, they realize that 100 percent of the time, they can't expect results. This mindset is helpful for entrepreneurs as they face many obstacles when they launch a new.

There is no question that the most aggressive players in each area will try a way to achieve a strategic edge. Athletes follow the rules of the game. Yet those who make the most significant long-term results are often well mindful of the need to work under such vital constraints. While most rivals search for an enduring legacy, they tend to leave it unaffected by controversy. Sure, a certain degree of scandal wills still enterprise the most widely popular people. Still, there is an enormous contrast in the complicated disposition of Steve Jobs and Bernie Madoff's acts.

Entrepreneurs are real rivals in the sense that they do not quickly succeed in building up their brands. Adherence to existing legislation allows SMEs to innovate and perform without jeopardizing their credibility.

What is relevant to the success of small business owners and contractors? Sight, skill, and talent.

Many rivals, though, have the same features. The secret to beat the competition and to win is emotional, expressed in one's mindset, ultimately person regulated and without cash. That is true of other human activities, aside from entertainment, arts, and politics.

How much did the underdog team or player triumph over the talented rival? Perhaps the difference is a mindset.

These qualities will place you in the right position to achieve market success.

1. Get your business passion. Get love.

Job ought to be enjoyable. Your enthusiasm will help you to conquer tough times and inspire people to work for you. Desire cannot be taught. Passion cannot be shown. When it stops, then it will take some spare time in tough moments. If it's an hour or a week, take stock of the cause you started and why you want to be your boss. This will restore the fire.

2. Set an indicator of trust.

Citizens believe and want to work with trustworthy individuals with a society of honesty. The same happens to consumers.

3. Except for fundamental principles, be versatile.

This is a fact that the goals and tactics will evolve. This versatility is an intrinsic advantage of small business over big business. Nonetheless, don't gamble on fundamental principles because of the demand for immediate benefit.

4. Don't let failure anxiety hold you down.

Defeat is an opportunity to learn. All the same, risk investors would rather spend money in a person who attempted to found a business and did not succeed than in someone who never tried.

5. Take decisions in a timely fashion.

This is all right to use your instincts. Planning and thought are proper. Good. Yet degradation leads to lost opportunities.

6. You are the biggest asset of the organization.

Take care of yourself, take care of yourself. Your wellbeing is more critical than the enterprise's most costly device or equipment. You should not choose between your family or business, play, or job. Keep your body healthy and robust, which increases your internal outlook in effect.

7. Have your emotions under control. Control your emotions.

Don't take profit and waste it on expensive toys to please others. Build a war chest to address unforeseen demands or possibilities. It also ensures that new thoughts and feedback can be heard irrespective of how crazy they sound.

8. Know yourself.

You have to trust in yourself, in your business and prosper. This confidence is infectious to the employees, clients, owners, vendors, and everyone concerned.

9. Encourage and graciously welcome critique.

Enable your faults to be acknowledged. You have to continually try to convince the workers that it's all right — and necessary — to share their truthful views even though they disagree with the boss ' perspective. It would not be cut for specific people by only saying it once or including it in a mission statement.

10. Hold an ethical ethos at work.

Your workers will support you. It will also allow you to conquer your competition, mainly if your product or service is very similar.

11. Rebound from defeats quickly.

It will have a lot of ups and downs when you develop the business. Know how to undo and carry on. The history can't be reversed.

12. Move out of your comfort zone regularly to do something meaningful.

Many times, you are dissatisfied with the necessary technical improvements, workers, responsibilities, rivalry, etc. Often you and the enterprise have to venture out of your comfort zone to grow personally.

The positive attitudes mentioned above will resolve or minimize several organizational and leadership vulnerabilities. Anything can be experienced even from inside love. Taking the time to comment regularly on these qualities. You will be inspired to do something.

5.5 Enhancing Communication Skills

As a small business owner, you have been in a position to draw more and more prospective clients to your enterprise as one of the essential tasks in your career. You must also bring the interest of your clients.

You need them; you've got customers already. You would never be adequate for your small business. Due to this, the role is to draw customers 'interest continually.

Even if it can seem simple, more work is required.

You've got a business. You have a product or service, and now you need someone to understand, see, know that you are here and able to fix their nasty, dull, and customer-friendly issues.

The first step is to sketch them. While this does not guarantee your business success, it's the first step you have to take as an entrepreneur from your side.

Some possible rules that you should enforce to draw your future customers. Measures to bring interest to consumers

1. Plan on how to attract market clients. Sometimes you cannot schedule anything, but if you schedule various avenues and incentives to draw your future clients, you can adopt a much more coordinated strategy.
2. To draw them, using various networks. There should be multiple outlets for different businesses. It is an outstanding effort to check different systems to attract your prospective customers 'interest. Today, social media sites are critical. Facebook is the biggest forum, so use the Facebook marketing plan in six stages.
3. Take note to be patient. If you pay attention to your future clients, you are more likely to be compatible.
4. You need no passwords and notify your future clients of all that is important to them. The competition's going to

bother me. They're just going to copy my work. The contest is going to learn about my job. While promises can also be made, you have to take the gamble that prospective clients cannot rely on you without causing their actual pain or emotions.

5. Do not clone, be original. You will read, evaluate, and copy your competitors. You ought to be single. Uniqueness is the fastest way to attract prospective customers.

6. A proper identity must be established for your small enterprise. Here are three ways to increase the enterprise's brand recognition.

7. Be optimistic. What you think is not necessary, what the consumers believe is more important. You have to be rational about it.

8. Start talking to listen. The hearing will tell you what the other side needs to do, and you will have your attention if you know it, and you strike them in their actual 'want.' and more customers are expected for your service. Don't waste time without the consumer's organized strategy.

5.6 Building Effective Customer Relationship

The most important thing in entrepreneurship is to retain the most valuable enterprise clients.

- The only goal to develop a brand would be to preserve customer ties.
- Happy consumers are most likely to remain faithful and return as returning customers.
- Consumer loyalty services, rewards, and surveys should be tailored to your schedule as well as to your campaign priorities.

The most critical thing to draw and keep the most profitable enterprise clients in sales and marketing.

To do this, you need to build and execute a custom plan to create, promote, sustain, and improve customer ties. Your business only benefits as remaining customers 'revenue over time meets the expense of attracting and servicing customers.

The relationship between long-term market success and long-term consumer relationships is stable. On any point of the consumer life cycle, from consumer search to customer development, customer retention, and business expansion, sufficient businesses leverage. After developing a certain degree of confidence and comfort, most consumers tend to stay faithful to SMEs and their products.

The selection and retention of customers is just the start of the process of consumer relationships. Ideally, the business will target high valuation and a low chance of attrition. The prices of purchasing a new enterprise are much higher than those of maintaining a current enterprise.

An organization keeps its clients by providing the value proposition in the acquisition period of the customer's life cycle. This means that the client does not have to go further; this is the explanation for the best level of service. When your partnership with your customers is built on confidence, collaboration and collaboration, the consumer can respond more readily to your new ideas, try new products/services, and see you as a trusted long-term collaborator.

An experienced client owner knows that current consumer partnerships should be maintained. It is easier to upsell and re-sells your products/services to this new client if a strong working partnership is formed. If your business is rising, there is a strong possibility that your products/services will be increasingly needed.

During the development period of the consumer's life cycle, the main goal is to increase the interest of a current client. Most SMEs talk about a customer's "lifetime worth." Customer expansion plans typically focus on growing rising customer's share of expenditures by extending their product/service spectrum.

Whereas it is essential not to lose sight of the value of attracting new consumers continuously. In other words, you can place your enterprise's potential success at risk if it is too reliant on anybody or even a few current customers. Be aware that the increase of transactions by one or more buyers does not reflect too much of the overall revenue of your product. This is important to strike a balance between servicing existing customers and attracting new customers.

Customer relationship management

Customers are undoubtedly one of the critical influences in launching a profitable enterprise and retaining it. Without customers — especially those who come back to employ you over and again — your enterprise will not survive. Therefore, the more you appreciate and establish relationships with your customers, the more successful you will be in growing your small enterprise.

1. Client needs

Not only can it help you build good partnerships with your clients from a communications standpoint, but it also lets you predict client desires and create continuous changes to enhance the enterprise across time.

When you have time to consider the needs of your clients, you would be best able to achieve consumer loyalty with your goods or services. You may also increase referrals and improve word-of-mouth marketing. Few ways which can enhance client relationships are

2. Coming to Know Your Clients

Even if you believe you understand your clients and their needs well, you can be surprised by the many ways in which you can get to know them best. Try making your discussions get a little personal by discussing what you do when you are off-hours, family information, etc. It does not have to be invasive, but exchanging details without research will improve relationships with the customers at times.

3. Do Outstanding Work

The consistency of the work must be excellent when building links. If you don't leave your buyers happy, long-term relationships can be nearly difficult to create. To meet your needs as much as possible and show how you will become a successful extension of the SMEs of your clients.

4. Communicate frequently with your customers

In all relationships, especially with your customers, accurate and efficient contact is essential. You will build the habit of good communication by receipt of customer calls and e-mails, arranging daily check-in, exchanging business news, and, as necessary, engaging with your customers through social media. You should be in close touch and keep your clients in the loop.

It is necessary to seek customer input during specific projects or in the event of achievements in long-term projects. You may use a customer service survey to take a formal approach or question them informally during a chat. Nonetheless, the first move in seeking customer input is to develop a strategy to resolve any complaints or suggestions and dedicate yourself to enhance management processes.

5. Your experience

Your clients accept and enjoy feedback several times on a more natural or more effective way of doing stuff. Using your knowledge of the work you do with your organization and your expertise to help your customers create solutions that fulfill their initial requirements. This can be achieved by detailed or even more casual consulting, such as exchanging ideas, advice, and tools to support the clients in their own SMEs.

By treating each customer relationship as an on-going collaboration, you will move the connection to a reciprocal, mutually beneficial cooperation. This emphasis will allow you to develop a healthy partnership rather than just do the job and move on.

These tips help you improve customer relations and build a stable base for your enterprise to expand to new heights.

Conclusion

Progress (the reverse of failure) is the state of an aim or task reached and accomplished. To excel requires fulfilling the desired goals and intended targets. In comparison, a certain social standing may be an achievement that represents a wealthy citizen, often famous for its beneficial outcomes. "Gaining money, popularity and renown" is the dictionary's definition of achievement.

You are the only one who can answer the above question.no one else can and recommend the definitive concept of performance, as it is not valid. Everybody feels differently about being successful in life and views success in a particular way, so there cannot be a concept suitable to everyone. You must know how to describe life's success! Make yourself mindful of what accomplishment, prosperity, and happiness of your entire life mean to you. Others may characterize success as possessing expensive cars and a large home, while others see a comfortable and healthy life with their families as the true definition of success. If you have found out what is important to you, you will work on your dreams and ambitions.

Some of the primary keys to progress in your career understand the importance of achievement in your personal life. The real sense of success goes way beyond traditional meanings of success, such as a lot of wealth, abundance, tangibility, and a lot of grades. Just the opposite: real success in life cannot be judged by the above-listed causes, but by the number of people who will lead a happier and more developed life because of what you have made.

That's the importance of performance. Individuals don't win prizes in their lives. Media and culture frequently believe that leading a good life requires becoming incredibly affluent and possessing other material items.

Yet success is about living a happier life and making this planet a safer place for everyone.

Is the concept of success a luxury sports car?

Contrary to success, failure means failure when attempting to accomplish objectives or targets. In addition to this standard concept of failure, even wealthy and productive people struggle in their lives. Think of the rich and famous, their scandals, addictions, and suicides. They were both excellent men, but many were still deeply dissatisfied with their life and did not see the importance of achievement. Wealth cannot be determined by money but by qualities that make you a happier person, including love, relationships, and your family.

What do you think? What do you think? Is it fair to sum up the right individual based on wealth, favor, or eminence?

The trouble with this definition of success (or any concept) is that success is subjective. Not every productive individual gains money, favor, or eminence. Many people are searching for things like equality, moral salvation, self-discipline, or decent people relationships.

There are several different ways to evaluate the right individual. Finally, you will determine the performance.

In the corporate world, more people are doing corporate by themselves, as they want independence from the manager, freedom from 9-to-5, or the right to work under their circumstances.

Yet many people in business eventually continue to follow the concept of success by Merriam-Webster in favor of their own: money, the home, the automobile.

Something is fundamentally wrong with these things, but I have found that most people in business desire nothing than wealth and recognition to be recognized.

However, this is still the path other people in business have followed.

We soon remember that it's not taking us where we want to go. It's like wasting years scaling a ladder to see the ladder just leaned against the wrong wall.

Why are so many people seeking milestones that don't please them? I think this happens when an entrepreneur never consciously determines how success feels.

The popularity of those that have wealth and prestige has, in many respects, been established, but that doesn't mean that they are the only ways to live that have an impact. Most people have real, exciting lives, but don't have much wealth or fame to prove them.

And how do you describe and step in this direction your version of success?

Take the time to see what you truly want.

If you struggle for a concept of your own, continue to ask yourself these questions: When did you feel pleased with your life? Who have you been with? What have you been doing? Which circumstances lead to your happiness? How do you use to replicate these moments?

When were you last pleased, pleased, and fulfilled? What did you look like that? Which of your wants, expectations, and aspirations has been met?

What are you most desire in life? Come up with a shortlist of things most important to you. What elements are more relevant in this list than the others? Place the items in order of priority, and, when you do, be frank.

Regardless of your responses, you may find that there is a lot more to this story than just wealth, power, and control. You will gain a much higher sense of the principles and the meaning of success once you know what's going on.

Work your principles together.

But if you've established how good yourself feels, it often takes a lot of concerted work to keep your expectations transparent to follow the traditional dictionary image that permeates our society.

Another significant risk is to ignore performance words that sound admirable, but do not belong on your importance list. For starters, if "giving up 50 percent of my revenue" (whatever that looks like) is not your highest expectations, don't include it in your concept of achievement.

Be truthful on what does and does not matter, as it would be much less complicated and exhausting if you encourage your real interests to demonstrate your concept of success.

When you describe how good your life is, note that you end up doing everything in life. The problem is, will you do these items deliberately on your own, or will you eventually survive because the people around you have chosen?

You have a lot to say. The best way to say what the job will be is to determine how successful the activities that will evaluate the progress of our SME are covered, to sum up, these in a brief analysis, allowing us to focus on our development.

Small business owners will do a great deal by preparing in advance to guarantee their success. The development of a strategic strategy is a crucial phase on the path to profitability for active business owners. Your clients are also worth learning and how to hit them through ads and different promotions. In the end, good businesses are determined by such criteria or measurements and their ethical behavior.

Loss is one of the most critical facets of corporate growth. Small enterprises that do not make a profit will inevitably collapse by the wayside.

As a small business owner, you will find a way to make a profit as quickly as possible. Another approach is to increase revenue and profits and offer goods or services with high enough costs. Determine unit costs to manufacture or purchase products and provide ample margin to make a reasonable profit. As an internet retailer, for example, you may choose to earn 20 percent more than your merchandise, job, and marketing expenses. Determine the price you equally divide and the 20% more element. You will also increase earnings by rising expenditures. Purchase wholesale only and rarely online. For starters, according to the online magazine "Entrepreneur," buy office equipment, which is gradually used to save money?

Your goods must be used frequently by customers; otherwise, a storm of returns would be expected. Please keep your pledges. As a manufacturer, check the products until they are put on the market and make prolonged use of them. You are using the measurements to set a reasonable timeline that will work for your goods. Regular use is one of the primary measurement points for items of good quality.

Active SMEs often respond to the demands of their customers through different features, colors, fragrances, sizes, or services. They are now growing dedicated consumers who tend to buy their products rather than rival brands. One of the most accessible opportunities for consumers to know is to question them. Marketing analysis surveys are one way to get reviews of this nature. Perform surveys by email, on the Internet, or in-person with consumers.

The sensitivity of Market Recognition is another measure of business success. Brand recognition is the percentage of individuals who, according to what you sell, know your name, goods, or services. Brand knowledge will be German for the regional sector.

As the owner of a small shop, for example, only the number of people who care about you in the neighborhood can be weighed. Brand identity-building takes time. Promoting your goods and services is one of the easiest ways to boost brand value. Publicity is one means of marketing goods. Many forms of creating brand recognition include promotional campaigns, trade fairs, interviews, publications, and special events.

Most productive small business owners donate to their families. Community donations Clear grants to a charity, or national protection support schemes are examples of charitable sacrifices.

References

1. The Surprising Truth About 'Success' and what it means for you. Retrieved from https://www.inc.com/young-entrepreneur-council/the-surprising-truth-about-success-what-it-means-for-you.html
2. Icehouse, T. The Psychology of the Entrepreneur. Retrieved from https://blog.theicehouse.co.nz/the-psychology-of-the-entrepreneur
3. The Meaning of Success and How to Define Success in Life. Retrieved from https://www.linkedin.com/pulse/meaning-success-how-define-life-eugene-adu-wusu
4. Feiffer, M. (2020). How Small-Business Owners Successfully Delegate HR. Retrieved from https://www.shrm.org/resourcesandtools/hr-topics/employee-relations/pages/how-small-business-owners-successfully-delegate-hr-.aspx
5. 3 Reasons A Competitive Spirit Is Critical For Entrepreneurs | Destroy Witt. (2015). Retrieved from https://thriveglobal.com/stories/3-reasons-a-competitive-spirit-is-critical-for-entrepreneurs-destry-witt/
6. Training, F., Us, A., Values, O., & Success, C. Leadership Skills You'll Need for Entrepreneurial Success - Foundry. Retrieved from https://foundr.com/leadership-skills-entrepreneurial-success
7. Gilman, L., McDaniel, C., Shah, A., Reece, M., Coffle, L., Talisman, B., & Hyatt, J. The Production Process: How Do We Make It?. Retrieved from https://opentextbc.ca/businessopenstax/chapter/the-production-process-how-do-we-make-it/
8. What are conversion costs? | Accounting Coach. Retrieved from https://www.accountingcoach.com/blog/what-are-conversion-costs

9. Retrieved from **https://smallbiztrends.com/2016/01/investment-tips-small-business.html**
10. Set, D., Box, L., Box, S., Plates, F., Cups, S., Bowls, S., & Bowls, C. The Importance of Eco-friendly Products - Kangaroo. Retrieved from **https://www.kangovou.com/the-importance-of-eco-friendly-products/**
11. Staff, E. How to Build a Brand Identity That Creates a High-Value Company. Retrieved from **https://www.entrepreneur.com/article/297774**
12. The challenges of growing a business - and how to meet them. Retrieved from **https://www.infoentrepreneurs.org/en/guides/the-challenges-of-growing-a-business---and-how-to-meet-them/**
13. Five small business tax deductions to keep in mind at tax time - Smart Company. Retrieved from **https://www.smartcompany.com.au/startupsmart/advice/business-planning/five-small-business-tax-deductions-to-keep-in-mind-at-tax-time/**
14. 7 Online Payment Services to Help Small Business Owners Get Paid. Retrieved from **https://www.thebalancesmb.com/5-online-payment-services-2951650**
15. Sutevski, D. How to Attract Customer's Attention?. Retrieved from **https://www.entrepreneurshipinabox.com/3975/how-to-attract-customers-attention/**

www.ingramcontent.com/pod-product-compliance
Lightning Source LLC
Chambersburg PA
CBHW052358220526
45465CB00003BB/1161